Especially for

_____

From

_____

Date

_____

THE
Wonder
OF CHRISTMAS

DANIEL PARTNER

BARBOUR
PUBLISHING

Cover and interior design: Greg Jackson, Thinkpen Design

Published by Barbour Publishing, Inc., P.O. Box 719, Uhrichsville, Ohio 44683
www.barbourbooks.com

*Our mission is to publish and distribute inspirational products offering exceptional value and
biblical encouragement to the masses.*

Member of the
Evangelical Christian
Publishers Association

Printed in China.

For Radina and Donn Welton
—with gratitude

But as touching brotherly love
ye need not that I write unto you.

1 Thessalonians 4:9

Contents

Introduction

What is Christmas? It seems to be a mere whirl of activity in which people shop, wrap, and give gifts; cook, serve, and eat food; go to parties, send Christmas cards, and drive around to see lights; attend movies, plays, and musical productions; and visit friends and family. Then, abruptly, the day after, it's all over until the next year.

"Christmas is about the birth of Jesus Christ," some will say. Others say that Christmas is for children, that it is a time for families to gather, or an occasion to help the needy. Merchants see it as a vital time for sales. It is all these. On the spiritual side, churches are crowded on Christmas Eve. But I've attended such services where Christ is hardly mentioned except in the standard hymns of the season and the gospel reading from Luke.

I think that the vital understanding of the birth of Christ has been buried by all these aspects of Christmas. So, I've written this book for anyone who desires to pause and remember the wonder of Christmas—Jesus Christ Himself.

Here are twenty-five days of readings drawn from scripture about the birth of Christ. Each day has a morning and an evening reading whose topics are related to the same set of verses. You would expect to read some of these verses in such a book, such as the familiar stories of Mary and Joseph, the wise men, and shepherds. But you may be surprised to see certain verses from Paul's epistles, the Old Testament prophets, or the book of Revelation. Even so, they all shed light on the meaning of the birth of Jesus Christ.

I hope this book will ignite in you a fresh revelation of Christ and that it will cause you, like the ancient shepherds of Bethlehem, to "see this thing which is come to pass, which the Lord hath made known unto us" (Luke 2:15).

Daniel Partner
Coos Bay, Oregon
November 2010

December 1

And so it was, that, while they were there,
the days were accomplished that she
should be delivered. And she brought
forth her firstborn son, and wrapped him
in swaddling clothes, and laid him in a
manger; because there was no room
for them in the inn.

LUKE 2:6–7

MORNING

While driving on US Route 3 through New Hampshire's north country toward Quebec, you enter the northernmost town in the state—Pittsburg. There in someone's dooryard is a small shed of weathered wood with an open front covered with chicken wire. Its year-round occupants are three-quarter-sized plastic figures of a man and a woman who are kneeling by a manger. It is a Christmas nativity scene. Year-round, hunters and fishers, loggers and truckers, natives and tourists pass by this display. It is most visible on long summer days when no colored lights surround the shed; when the bright sun and green grass contrast with this rendering of the birth of Jesus Christ typically seen in the dark of winter.

Theologians call Christ's birth the *Incarnation*.

The Gospel of John describes it like this: "The Word was made flesh, and dwelt among us" (1:14). The poet Ben Jonson (1572–1637), wrote of it in "A Hymn of the Nativity of My Savior": "I sing the birth, was born tonight / The author both of life and light." Our children sing, "Away in a manger, no crib for a bed," and a citizen of Pittsburg, New Hampshire, uses old planks, colored plastic, and chicken wire to tell of the birth of a child who was the Son of God.

But from the simplest to the most sublime, nothing we can do or say or sing can adequately represent this event.

[He] emptied himself, taking the form of a servant, being made in the likeness of men (Philippians 2:7 ASV, emphasis added). Crude chicken wire and well-crafted phrases are equally impotent to explain this. *Being found in fashion as a man, he humbled himself, becoming obedient even unto death* (v. 8). Use plastic or use poetry; try as you will,

nothing will do to completely describe it. Combine the voices of apostles, poets, theologians, and every children's choir on earth to sing the significance of the birth of Jesus Christ. Construct a cathedral, cobble together a crèche, or create a holiday called Christmas. Or better yet, each day of the year remember the wonder of Christ's birth, and pray, "Thank You, Father, that in the fulness of time, You sent forth Your Son" (see Galatians 4:4).

NIGHT

Whatever became of the overcrowded inn that could not receive Mary and Joseph on the eve of Jesus' birth?

Some ancient man built it of stone or bricks of clay, spread stucco across its walls, then hung shutters to cover its windows, tamped down the dirt floor firm and level, and attached a gate and door.

A man and a woman made that inn their home, prepared food and drink, and took in guests. Were its proprietors well known in town? Perhaps he was prominent in the synagogue and she was sought out by other women at the town's well. They may have had children and grandchildren. Could they have been pleased to turn away the man from Nazareth and his pregnant wife?

After the child who was to be king of the Jews was born in an outbuilding of the inn and taken far away to Egypt, King Herod's soldiers came to kill all the little boys in Bethlehem (Matthew 2:13–18). Who did the innkeepers lose to this slaughter? Grandsons, sons, nephews, and cousins all fell beneath the Roman blades. Grievous wailing must have echoed throughout that inn as family blood stained its courtyard.

What became of that inn? It is gone; it is dust. Not only is the inn dust, the innkeepers have returned to dust along with all the jars in their kitchen and guests in their rooms. Only one artifact remains to memorialize its existence—the record of the birth of Jesus Christ.

The story of Bethlehem's crowded inn is a parable of the Christmas season: Of all the gifts and gatherings that fill your heart this month, which of them will remain when you have returned to dust? The answer to this question kindles thanks to God for His indescribable gift (2 Corinthians 9:15). ✵

December 2

And in the sixth month the angel
Gabriel was sent from God unto a city
of Galilee, named Nazareth, to a virgin
espoused to a man whose name was
Joseph, of the house of David; and the
virgin's name was Mary. And the angel
came in unto her, and said, Hail, thou
that art highly favored, the Lord is with
thee: blessed art thou among women.

LUKE 1:26–28

MORNING

The Christmas story begins with the visit of the archangel Gabriel to a young woman. In his poem, "Mary and Gabriel," The English poet Rupert Brooke (1887–1915) described that appearing like this:

Young Mary, loitering once her garden way,
Felt a warm splendor grow in the April day,
As wine that blushes water through. And soon,
Out of the gold air of the afternoon,
One knelt before her: hair he had or fire,
Bound back above his ears with golden wire,
Baring the eager marble of his face.

Imagine the torrent of feelings that surged through Mary's heart at that moment. And then the angel spoke! "Fear not, Mary: for thou hast found favor with God. And, behold, thou shalt conceive in thy womb, and bring forth a son, and shalt call his name JESUS. He shall be great, and shall be called the Son of the Highest: and the Lord God shall give unto him the throne of his father David: And he shall reign over the house of Jacob for ever; and of his kingdom there shall be no end" (Luke 1:30–33). These words weren't spoken to a prophet, a leader, or an elder; this news came to a young woman for whom childhood was still a fresh memory.

It was Mary, an extraordinary personality, who first saw the light in the Christmas story. Too many Protestant Christians fail to appreciate Mary because the Roman Catholic Church took to calling her the Mother of God and the Queen of Heaven. This caused an unfortunate reaction that transferred Mary to the second-class coach of the gospel train.

But her significance cannot be described

by even the most ingenious title given by a most extravagant religion. God used Mary's obedience to give Christ His humanity. "When the fulness of the time came, God sent forth his Son, born of a woman" (Galatians 4:4 ASV). His humanity didn't come miraculously, through a snap of God's fingers. But, just as everyone emerged into this world through a woman, Christ came to us through Mary's pregnancy and pain of labor.

Mary's response to Gabriel tells of her importance in the gospel story: "Oh, how my soul praises the Lord. How my spirit rejoices in God my Savior! For he took notice of his lowly servant girl, and from now on all generations will call me blessed" (Luke 1:46–48 NLT).

NIGHT

Gabriel was busy at the beginning of Luke, appearing to two people and receiving from them two very different responses. The first appearance was to old Zechariah (Luke 1:11–20) and the other to young Mary (Luke 1:26–28).

When the angel told Zechariah that his elderly wife was to have a son, he responded, "How can I be sure of this? I am an old man and my wife is well along in years" (Luke 1:18 NIV). Zechariah couldn't accept the Lord's words, so he asked for a sign to prove them true. This was unbelief (Luke 1:19–20).

When Gabriel told Mary that she would have a child, she wondered, "But how can this happen? I am a virgin" (Luke 1:34 NLT). The angel informed her, "The Holy Ghost shall come upon thee, and the power of the Highest shall overshadow thee: therefore also that holy thing which shall be born of thee shall be called the Son of God" (Luke 1:35). Mary's response to Gabriel shows her to be the first New Testament believer. She said, "Behold the handmaid of the Lord; be it unto me according to thy word" (Luke 1:38). This response came out of faith, the faith that verifies the unseen things of God (Hebrews 11:1).

Rupert Brooke ended his poem about the appearance of Gabriel to Mary like this:

The great wings were spread
Showering glory on the fields, and fire.
The whole air, singing, bore him up, and higher,
Unswerving, unreluctant. Soon he shone
A gold speck in the gold skies; then was gone.
The air was colder, and gray. She stood alone.

This Christmas season recall the woman who gave birth to the Son of God while giving His believers their first example of the faith that needs no outward verification, "For we walk by faith, not by sight" (2 Corinthians 5:7). ❄

December 3

And Mary said, My soul doth magnify the Lord, and my spirit hath rejoiced in God my Savior. For he hath regarded the low estate of his handmaiden: for, behold, from henceforth all generations shall call me blessed. For he that is mighty hath done to me great things; and holy is his name. And his mercy is on them that fear him from generation to generation. He hath shewed strength with his arm; he hath scattered the proud in the imagination of their hearts. He hath put down the mighty from their seats, and exalted them of low degree. He hath filled the hungry with good things; and the rich he hath sent empty away. He hath helped his servant Israel, in remembrance of his mercy; as he spake to our fathers, to Abraham, and to his seed for ever.

LUKE 1:46–55

MORNING

Gabriel appeared to young Mary and told her that God would, through her, bring forth the Savior of the world. Not surprisingly, at first Mary "was greatly troubled at his words" (Luke 1:29 NIV).

Soon she hurried to the hill country of Judea to visit her cousin Elizabeth, Zechariah's wife. Certainly, as she traveled, Mary considered what had happened and repeated the angel's words over and over in her mind. At some point the significance of it all dawned on her. As she entered Elizabeth's house, Mary exclaimed, "My soul doth magnify the Lord, and my spirit hath rejoiced in God my Savior" (Luke 1:46– 47). Then, in a rich soliloquy, she described God's purpose in the birth of Christ. This portion of scripture is called "Mary's Song" or the "Magnificat" after the first word of the Latin translation (Luke 1:46–55).

Consider the effect the words of God had upon Mary. Before, she was merely "a virgin espoused to a man whose name was Joseph" (Luke 1:27). Scholars say that she was probably in her early teens. If so, she must have been shy. But suddenly she is bold, proclaiming without hesitation, "My soul doth magnify the Lord, and my spirit hath rejoiced in God my Savior." Surely she had been unsure of herself as the betrothed of an older man, but no more. "Behold, from henceforth all generations shall call me blessed" (Luke 1:48), she says. Her confidence overflows as she proclaims, "He that is mighty hath done to me great things; and holy is his name" (Luke 1:49).

The girl has been transformed into a prophet on par with the greatest of Israel. In God's name she condemns the proud and wealthy, has compassion on the poor, and invokes the name of the illustrious Abraham. This is the effect that the Word of God can have on any soul—even yours.

Gabriel spoke only about 150 words for Mary to ponder. You and I have the entire Bible to consider. Not only so, "Long ago God spoke many times and in many ways to our ancestors through the prophets. And now in these final days, *he has spoken to us through his Son*" (Hebrews 1:1–2 NLT, emphasis added).

NIGHT

You'd think that Mary would have been weary after the journey to her cousin's house. Instead, she was invigorated and filled with the Spirit because of the words of God that she heard from Gabriel. With energy and passion, Mary spoke of God's ways.

We, too, can be invigorated by the meaning of Christmas. Yet, most everyone complains of feeling exhausted by the Christmas season. The activities can wear down the body, and the shopping can drain the bank account. But read Mary's Song. It explains the actual reason for such experiences: "He hath scattered the proud in the imagination of their hearts" (Luke 1:51). People who hope to find satisfaction in Christmas gifts and foods and gatherings are scattered, weakened in the imagination of our hearts.

Now don't get me wrong. I'm not like those Puritans of old who attempted to ban the observance of Christmas. I like it when the cheerful holiday lights appear in the darkness of winter; I'm happy to be invited to a gathering of friends where I can indulge in some special foods; and there's nothing like getting a gift from someone who loves me. But I have to be careful that my imagination doesn't run away with me. I've been scattered too many times by expecting satisfaction in such things.

Mary sings, "He hath filled the hungry with good things; and the rich he hath sent empty away" (Luke 1:53). If you become exhausted by the Christmas season, ask yourself, "Have I been filled with good things, or is God sending me away empty?"

Again, I am not proposing that anyone cease the celebration of Christmas. I only hope that believers add to it the remembrance of God's mercy. Daily in the hustle and bustle of the season—in the grocery, at the mall, in sending greeting cards, and gathering gifts—please consider the thing that occupied and energized Mary as she traveled to Elizabeth's—she would be with child and give birth to a son, give Him the name Jesus, and He will be called the Son of the Most High. "The Lord God will give him the throne of his ancestor David. And he will reign over Israel forever; his Kingdom will never end!" (Luke 1:32–33 NLT). See if this fills you with the good things of Christmas. ❋

December 4

When they had heard the king,
they departed; and, lo, the star, which
they saw in the east, went before them,
till it came and stood over where the
young child was. When they saw the star,
they rejoiced with exceeding great joy.
And when they were come into the house,
they saw the young child with Mary his
mother, and fell down, and worshipped
him: and when they had opened their
treasures, they presented unto him gifts;
gold, and frankincense and myrrh.

MATTHEW 2:9–11

Morning

The English poet Christina Rossetti (1830–1894) wrote the lyrics to a most beautiful and meaningful Advent hymn. It begins:

In the bleak midwinter, frosty wind made moan,
Earth stood hard as iron, water like a stone;
Snow had fallen, snow on snow, snow on snow,
In the bleak midwinter, long ago.

The poet imagines the conditions surrounding Christ's birth. It is a gray, cold midwinter day. Outside, the wind moans, the earth is iron-hard, water is frozen solid, and everywhere is "snow on snow, snow on snow." Since this is a poem, it does not pretend to describe the actual weather conditions in Bethlehem at the time Jesus was born. But it does truthfully portray the human state and the condition of our souls without Christ Jesus. These four lines tell of the earth's desperate need to be warmed by God's love.

Rossetti uses the next stanzas of the poem to beautifully express how out of place our Savior was in this setting. She observes that heaven cannot hold God nor can earth sustain Him, yet in the bleak midwinter, a stable sufficed as the birthplace of God's Son.

In the end Christina Rossetti tells of the earnest impulse of those who realize who Jesus is:

What can I give Him, poor as I am?
If I were a shepherd, I would bring a lamb;
If I were a wise man, I would do my part;
Yet what I can I give Him: give my heart.

Her gift, like the birth of Christ, is entirely out of the ordinary, yet absolutely necessary. The shepherd's lamb and the magi's precious gifts for the Christ-child were useful at the time, no doubt. But do you possess anything that God really needs? No one does. Yet, you do have one thing that He wants.

This is the season of gift buying, gift wrapping, and gift giving. As the many presents pass from hand to hand, pause and ask yourself the poet's question, "What can I give to God, poor as I am?" You may give your money or your time, but these merely point toward the only thing God desires—your heart.

NIGHT

We know the wise men presented wonderful gifts to Jesus, but I wonder if they knew the significance their gifts held.

Henry Wadsworth Longfellow (1807–1882) wrote a poem about these magi titled "The Three Kings." Concerning their gifts, he wrote:

They laid their offerings at His feet:
The gold was their tribute to a King,
The frankincense, with its odor sweet,
Was for the Priest, the Paraclete,
The myrrh for the body's burying.

The myrrh indicates the death of Christ by which we are justified from sin (Romans 6:6–7). Myrrh was commonly used when preparing a body for burial. Nicodemus used roughly one hundred pounds of embalming ointment made from myrrh and aloes when he buried Jesus (John 19:39). Myrrh is plant resin and is harvested by cutting through the bark of a tree. This cutting is evocative of the Lord's experience on the cross when a soldier pierced his side (John 19:34).

The frankincense is symbolic of Christ's priesthood, since the priests of Israel offered incense in worship and the offering of the sacrifices. "He is the kind of high priest we need," scripture declares, "because he is holy and blameless" (Hebrews 7:26 NLT). Since frankincense, like myrrh, is a plant resin, it, too, indicates Christ's death. Longfellow says that frankincense also symbolizes the Paraclete. This is the Holy Spirit as the Comforter who, like a fragrance, brings Christ to our remembrance (John 14:26).

Gold is a gift for a king, true enough. But it also indicates that this little boy, whom the magi came to worship, was God's Son. Gold is often used in scripture as a symbol for God such as in Job 22:23–25 (NIV) which says, "If you return to the Almighty, you will be restored. . . . Then the Almighty will be your gold, the choicest silver for you." The fact that gold does not corrode shows Christ's purity and incorruptibility. It is the also most malleable and ductile of all metals—one ounce of gold can be beaten into a three-hundred-square-foot sheet of foil. This is suggestive of Christ's flexibility as He is patient and forgiving of us.

Gold, frankincense, and myrrh. These three precious gifts brought by magi to an obscure Middle Eastern place reveal who was living there—it was the redeeming Savior and High Priest who was the very God of the universe! ❄

December 5

Now when Jesus was born in Bethlehem
of Judaea in the days of Herod the king,
behold, there came wise men from the
east to Jerusalem, saying, Where is he that
is born King of the Jews? for we have
seen his star in the east, and are
come to worship him.

MATTHEW 2:1–2

Morning

Henry Wadsworth Longfellow was an American poet and linguist. He is best known as the author of "Paul Revere's Ride" and "The Song of Hiawatha." Several of his lesser-known works were written on Christian subjects.

His poem "The Three Kings," quoted in yesterday's reading, romanticizes the original story of the wise men as found in Matthew 2:1–12. Beginning with its title, the poem expresses many modern-day misconceptions about these men, such as the idea that there were three of them. Its first three stanzas describe the wise men as richly dressed and traveling at night by starlight. But the Bible does not give us this much detail about them. No one knows who these men were, where they came from, or how many of them made the journey.

The star they followed is even more of a mystery. It led them as far as Jerusalem, where the travelers seem to have lost sight of it. So, they went to King Herod and asked him, "Where is he that is born King of the Jews?" (Matthew 2:2). Herod had no idea what to tell them, so he called in the priests and religious teachers of Jerusalem. They knew exactly where Christ was to be born, referring to Micah 5:2, saying, "But thou, Bethlehem Ephratah, though thou be little among the thousands of Judah, yet out of thee shall he come forth unto me that is to be ruler in Israel; whose goings forth have been from of old, from everlasting" (Matthew 2:5–6).

These religious men knew these strangers had come to find the long-awaited Messiah. However, if there was a possibility that the Christ could be found at that moment in nearby Bethlehem, why didn't they go with the travelers and seek Him out? Instead, they did nothing. Although this story is baffling, this much is known: those who should have welcomed the Messiah missed their opportunity, while foreigners traveled far to honor the King of the Jews.

That was long ago. Today, church and culture have combined to create an entire season of the year in which Jesus Christ is supposed to be honored. But if some dusty strangers arrived at your Christmas Eve service hoping to find the Christ, where would you direct their search, and would you go along with them in hope of finding the Lord?

NIGHT

The wise men lived at the time of the Lord's first appearing, yet their story tells something about His second coming. Two lessons emerge from the magi's encounter with the religious leaders in Jerusalem.

First, these priests and scribes knew the verse well that tells where the Messiah would appear, yet they didn't go to Bethlehem to find Him. This shows that Bible knowledge alone will never secure our preparedness to meet the Lord. Yes, it is good to know the scriptural prophecies and promises about the Lord. However, it is better to love the Lord. Such love causes a longing to see Him face-to-face.

The second lesson we learn from the magi's encounter with the religious leaders of Jerusalem is that faith and politics do not mix.

Something Jesus said in a later context explains this: "No servant can serve two masters: for either he will hate the one, and love the other; or else he will hold to the one, and despise the other" (Luke 16:13).

Those religious leaders were in collusion with Herod, the political power of the day. To go to Bethlehem, they would have had to leave behind their earthly master, Herod, in order to find their heavenly one. This was risky. They decided they had too much to lose in the way of comfort, prestige, and power, so they stayed home.

I think certain church leaders today should learn this lesson from Herod's religious leaders, who chose to serve their earthly master over God's Son. If they would transfer their hope from politics to the appearing of Christ, the world would greatly benefit. And they, like Paul, could boast, "I have kept the faith: Henceforth there is laid up for me a crown of righteousness, which the Lord, the righteous judge, shall give me at that day: and not to me only, but unto all them also that love his appearing" (2 Timothy 4:7–8). ❊

December 6

And the Word was made flesh, and dwelt among us, (and we beheld his glory, the glory as of the only begotten of the Father,) full of grace and truth.

JOHN 1:14

MORNING

When I was a little boy and appeared in my Sunday school's Christmas pageant, I played a shepherd. This role was given to children who were too young to play the glamorous characters like Mary, Joseph, angels, and wise men. There must have been at least a dozen of us traipsing and tripping down the aisle of the church that night. I remember that my turban was an actual bath towel and my robe was the same bed sheet that had formerly transformed me into a ghost on Halloween.

The script of our Christmas pageant was based on the stories told in the Gospels of Matthew and Luke. These accounts tell of the action surrounding the birth of Jesus Christ. But the Gospel of John cuts through these descriptive accounts and simply tells the significance of what happened. John's account provides no opportunity to fall into sentimentality or nostalgia about Christmas. Neither does it lend itself to pageants on Christmas Eve.

The Bible has much to say about the flesh and the significance of Christ becoming flesh. Flesh is humanity at its weakest, so Christ was "crucified through weakness" (2 Corinthians 13:4). Flesh is mortal and dying humanity, "a wind that passeth away, and cometh not again" (Psalm 78:39). Thus Christ was "put to death in the flesh" (1 Peter 3:18). Flesh is humanity tainted with sin (Colossians 2:13), so the perfectly holy Son of God appeared "in the likeness of sinful flesh" (Romans 8:3), and was made the sin offering for us (2 Corinthians 5:21). The man we celebrate this Christmas season was, by His birth, perfectly enabled to condemn sin in the flesh (Romans 8:3) and the wonder of Christmas is that He chose to become flesh in order to submit to death and save us from sin.

NIGHT

This is the wonder of Christmas, that the Word was made flesh and dwelt among us. He took upon Himself the likeness of humanity and lived in the same world as us, under the same conditions. He had been with the Father before the world was, yet came to earth to live with us.

The Bible says that the Word "dwelt among us" (John 1:14). These words literally mean that He *tabernacled* among us. Since a tabernacle is a tent, this reminds us that He lived in low circumstances, like the common man, here on earth. Much like shepherds caring for their sheep live in tents, so did the good Shepherd (John 10:11). Soldiers in the field also live in tents, and when Christ was born, He took to the battlefield, set up His standard, and pitched

His tent—a human body in which He successfully fought a war against God's adversary (Luke 4:1–14).

When Christ lived among us, He took the way of the patriarchs who by faith lived in the land of promise like it was a foreign country, dwelling in tents and confessing that they were strangers and pilgrims on the earth (Hebrews 11:9, 13).

Of even more significance is the fact that in ancient days God dwelt in an elaborate tent, the tabernacle, built by Moses (Exodus 29:42–43). Today, God is seen in Jesus Christ. In the days of Moses, the high priest went into the tabernacle to meet with God. Today we encounter God through Christ. Not only so, God, who spoke to Israel from the tabernacle, "has in these last days spoken to us by His Son" (Hebrews 1:2 NKJV).

The incarnation of God in Christ is beyond explanation, but images such as these help us to understand it a little. Here is one final, glorious picture: The tabernacle held the two tablets upon which was written God's law—the law that was impossible to keep (Romans 8:3). In contrast, John tells us the good news that the tent named Jesus Christ is full of grace and truth to all who believe (John 1:14). ❄

December 7

And when they were departed, behold, the angel
of the Lord appeareth to Joseph in a dream, saying,
Arise, and take the young child and his mother,
and flee into Egypt, and be thou there until I bring
thee word: for Herod will seek the young child to
destroy him. . . . Then Herod, when he saw that he
was mocked of the wise men, was exceeding wroth,
and sent forth, and slew all the children that were
in Bethlehem, and in all the coasts thereof, from two
years old and under, according to the time which
he had diligently inquired of the wise men. Then
was fulfilled that which was spoken by Jeremiah the
prophet, saying, In Rama was there a voice heard,
lamentation, and weeping, and great mourning,
Rachel weeping for her children, and would not be
comforted, because they are not.

MATTHEW 2:13, 16–18

Morning

At the time of Jesus' birth, who knew that the promised Savior had been born? Mary, Joseph, Elizabeth, and some shepherds were probably the only ones. Herod the Great got the news that a king had been born in his realm through strangers from the East—the wise men. Though it was hardly more than hearsay, Herod took the news seriously. He feared any political rival, even a newborn baby. Out of this fear came the infamous slaughter of the innocents described in Matthew 2:16–18.

The English composer William Byrd (1543–1623) also memorialized this tragedy. Many consider Byrd the greatest English composer of any age, and some judge him the greatest composer of the Renaissance. Here is the first verse of his song to the little Jesus, "Lulla, My Sweet Little Baby":

Lulla, la lulla, lulla lullaby.
My sweet little baby, what meanest Thou to cry?
Be still my blessed babe, though cause Thou hast
*   of mourn,*
Whose blood most innocent to shed the cruel king
*   hath sworn.*
And lo, alas, behold what slaughter he doth make,
Shedding the blood of infants all, sweet Savior, for
*   Thy sake.*
A King is born, they say, which King this king
*   would kill.*
Oh woe, and woeful heavy day, when wretches
*   have their will!*

Although composed in the form of a lullaby, this is a lament over the "woeful heavy day, when wretches have their will." When I look around the world today, a similar lament rises in my heart because wretches like King Herod still conduct royal intrigue and mass murder.

But this season of the celebration of Jesus' birth holds the hope of His second coming. For just as Herod's bloody rage could not prevent Christ's birth, so also nothing can hinder His return!

If you are like me and sometimes grieve that latter-day Herods still slaughter the innocents, remember the Lord's promise, "Blessed are they that mourn: for they shall be comforted" (Matthew 5:4). And, amidst the feasts and lights of Christmas, offer this prayer for the second coming: "How long, O Lord, holy and true?" (Revelation 6:10).

NIGHT

Consider the setting of William Byrd's poem: An angel appears to Joseph and says, "Arise, and take the young child and his mother, and flee into Egypt, and be thou there until I bring thee word: for Herod will seek the young child to destroy him" (Matthew 2:13). Joseph arises in the dark of night, lights a lamp, rouses his wife, and whispers to her the angel's urgent, dreamlike message. They move quickly about the room, dressing, packing, planning. What do they take for the trip to Egypt? What must they abandon in Bethlehem?

Then the child awakens. Joseph kneels by Jesus' little cot. "Lulla, la lulla, lulla lullaby," he sings in a whisper, his lips brushing the boy's warm forehead. Then Joseph tells God's Son what is to occur:

Lulla, la lulla, lulla lullaby.
My sweet little baby, what meanest Thou to cry?
Lo, my little babe, be still, lament no more;
From fury Thou shalt step aside, help have we still
in store.
We heavenly warning have some other soil to seek,
From death must fly the Lord of life, as lamb both
mild and meek.
Thus must my babe obey the king that would
Him kill.
Oh woe, and woeful heavy day, when wretches
have their will.

Joseph's song to Jesus, as imagined by Byrd, remembers the extraordinary events of the boy's short life. He sings of the slaughter that is soon to come upon Bethlehem—a lullaby of murder and martyrdom. He weaves into the melody the strange story of the visitors from the East, whose gifts would soon be sold to finance the family's flight to safety. He recounts the shepherds' hurried visit—those rough men who were the first of the human race to hear of the Savior's birth.

"Lulla, la lulla, lulla lullaby. My sweet little baby, what meanest Thou to cry?" The baby had plenty to cry about. While Joseph sang of the lovely mother who was to nurture "the Son of heavenly seed," armed soldiers were assembling nearby, preparing to kill Him. But all the while Joseph lilted the prophecies foretelling the baby's kingly life and reign and hustled the bundled mother and son out of Bethlehem toward Egypt—"Lulla, la lulla, lulla lullaby." ❄

December 8

Let this mind be in you, which was also in Christ Jesus: Who, being in the form of God, thought it not robbery to be equal with God: But made himself of no reputation, and took upon him the form of a servant, and was made in the likeness of men: And being found in fashion as a man, he humbled himself, and became obedient unto death, even the death of the cross. Wherefore God also hath highly exalted him, and given him a name which is above every name: That at the name of Jesus every knee should bow, of things in heaven, and things in earth, and things under the earth; And that every tongue should confess that Jesus Christ is Lord, to the glory of God the Father.

PHILIPPIANS 2:5–11

Morning

This is as close as the apostle Paul comes to a Christmas story. But he cannot stop with the birth of Jesus; the apostle was compelled to review the entire progress of Christ's life. Here is described the birth, life, death, resurrection, ascension, and second coming of the Lord. The essence of the four Gospels and the book of Revelation are compressed into the above 131 words of the King James Version. At this time of year it is worthwhile to consider the outcome of the birth of Christ.

The apostles tell us who Jesus was: "Being in the form of God, [he] thought it not robbery to be equal with God" (Philippians 2:6). This is just as Matthew reported, "They shall call his name Emmanuel, which being interpreted is, God with us" (1:23). Or John who said, "In the beginning was the Word. . .and the Word was God" (1:1). But Jesus did not cling to His equality with God when He appeared on the earth, and when people saw Him, they had no idea who He really was.

The Savior didn't appear in a divine form. Rather the Son of God laid aside His glory and "made himself of no reputation, and took upon him the form of a servant, and was made in the likeness of men" (Philippians 2:7). These words describe what happened when Jesus emerged from Mary's womb. As John said, "The Word was made flesh" (John 1:14).

Then, for some thirty years, Christ was "found in fashion as a man" (Philippians 2:8). In other words, He was no angel. He was indistinguishable from all other men. When Joseph brought Mary and the boy back from Egypt, "he went and lived in a town called Nazareth. So was fulfilled what was said through the prophets, that He would be called a Nazarene" (Matthew 2:23 NIV). Not a god or a guru, simply a Nazarene.

A lovely hymn expresses the wonder of Christmas. It was written by William Young Fullerton (1857–1932) and is sung to the tune "Londonderry Air" (the melody of "Danny Boy"). Here is the first verse of this hymn:

I cannot tell why He whom angels worship,
Should set His love upon the sons of men,
Or why, as Shepherd, He should seek
    the wanderers,
To bring them back, they know not how or when.
But this I know, that He was born of Mary
When Bethlehem's manger was His only home,
And that He lived at Nazareth and labored,
And so the Savior, Savior of the world is come.

NIGHT

God humbled Himself to become a man. What infinite condescension! But this is not all; "He humbled himself, and became obedient unto death, even the death of the cross" (Philippians 2:8). He not only took the form of man but the mortality of the flesh—and died the most shameful and painful of all deaths, the death of crucifixion.

The magi's gift of myrrh, an embalming spice, pointed toward this death (Matthew 2:11). And the prophet Simeon told Mary of Jesus' death, saying, "Behold, this child is set for the fall and rising again of many in Israel; and for a sign which shall be spoken against" (Luke 2:34).

William Fullerton's hymn tells of Christ's death in more simple phrases:

I cannot tell how silently He suffered,
As with His peace He graced this place of tears,
Or how His heart upon the cross was broken,
The crown of pain to three and thirty years.
But this I know, He heals the brokenhearted,
And stays our sin, and calms our lurking fear,
And lifts the burden from the heavy laden,
For yet the Savior, Savior of the world is here.

Because Jesus obediently died such a death, God lifted Him up from the grave to the heavens, gave all power into His hands (Matthew 28:18), and made the humble name *Jesus* a name above every name (Philippians 2:10–11).

The incurious Jewish leaders of Jerusalem predicted this would happen, quoting to Herod the words of their own prophet: "And thou Bethlehem, in the land of Juda, art not the least among the princes of Juda: for out of thee shall come a Governor, that shall rule my people Israel" (Matthew 2:6).

No less an authority, Gabriel told Mary, "He shall be great, and shall be called the Son of the Highest: and the Lord God shall give unto him the throne of his father David: And he shall reign over the house of Jacob for ever; and of his kingdom there shall be no end" (Luke 1:32–33).

And so Fullerton sings,

I cannot tell how He will win the nations,
How He will claim His earthly heritage,
How satisfy the needs and aspirations
Of East and West, of sinner and of sage.
But this I know, all flesh shall see His glory,
And He shall reap the harvest He has sown,
And some glad day His sun shall shine in splendor
When He the Savior, Savior of the world is known. ❇

December 9

And there were in the same country
shepherds abiding in the field,
keeping watch over their flock by night.
And, lo, the angel of the Lord came upon
them, and the glory of the Lord shone
round about them: and they were sore
afraid. And the angel said unto them,
Fear not: for, behold, I bring you good
tidings of great joy, which shall be to all
people. For unto you is born this day
in the city of David a Saviour,
which is Christ the Lord.

LUKE 2:8–11

MORNING

I wonder if the shepherds were thinking about God that night of Christ's birth. It's possible that they were pious men who took advantage of the night watches to pray. Might they have been considering, hoping for, the birth of their Messiah?

These weren't the only shepherds in the Bible to receive a message from God. Long before them, another shepherd was tending a flock on the back side of the Sinai desert. He doesn't seem to have been thinking of God at all. Still, the angel of the Lord appeared to Moses in a flame of fire from the midst of a bush. Moses' experience with that messenger marked the beginning of Israel's salvation from Egyptian bondage (Exodus 3:1–12).

The shepherds near Bethlehem didn't see

anything so simple as a burning bush. The glory of the Lord was *all around them* and these hardworking men were afraid. As the angel was trying to calm them down, "Suddenly there was. . .a multitude of the heavenly host praising God, and saying, Glory to God in the highest, and on earth peace, good will toward men" (Luke 2:13–14). Imagine how this amazed them.

It is a credit to the courage and faith of these rough shepherds that they said to each other, "Let us now go even unto Bethlehem, and see this thing which is come to pass, which the Lord hath made known unto us" (Luke 2:15). So they went looking for the sign—a "babe wrapped in swaddling clothes, lying in a manger" (Luke 2:12). How ordinary. This is like the dry desert bush that Moses saw. This is the way the Savior of the world was introduced.

After they had found Mary, Joseph, and Jesus, the shepherds told others what had happened and "all they that heard it wondered at those things" (Luke 2:18).

God rarely communicates through angels or flames. The next time this happens, Jesus Christ will come again to be "revealed from heaven with his mighty angels" (2 Thessalonians 1:7). Meanwhile, let's seek Him in an ordinary way. Like shepherds with a manger or a bush, let us find Him in prayer and within the pages of the Bible.

NIGHT

Christ has already been born, lived His life, and accomplished God's plan. So we can easily understand the words that predicted His birth. Isaiah makes perfect sense to us when he says, "Behold, a virgin shall conceive, and bear a son, and shall call his name Immanuel" (7:14). And, Micah 5:2 makes it obvious to us where the Messiah was to be born: "But thou, Bethlehem Ephratah, though thou be little among the thousands of Judah, yet out of thee shall he come forth unto me that is to be ruler in Israel; whose goings forth have been from of old, from everlasting."

But it wasn't so easy for people living two thousand years ago to understand these things. The Jewish leaders in Jerusalem didn't go with the wise men to seek the newborn

King. Similarly, the people in Bethlehem who heard the news from the shepherds apparently didn't go to see Him either. In fact, most of the people in Israel missed out on the Lord's first appearing.

Believers in Christ can be thankful to God that they have seen the meaning of the birth of Christ. We did not miss it. Now we wait for a second appearing of Jesus Christ. What shall we do until He comes? We can care for the poor, preach the gospel, and work for justice. Plus, the Lord Himself tells us of the one thing He would like to find when He returns.

Luke 18:1–17 tells two parables about prayer. Tucked between the two is this half-verse: "Nevertheless when the Son of man cometh, shall he find faith on the earth?" (Luke 18:8). We each must answer this question for ourselves.

I don't think these parables mean we all

must be on our knees actively praying at the moment the Lord appears. What it does mean is that we should have an attitude of the heart that is inclined toward the Lord (1 Kings 8:58). We can join the apostle who completed his life knowing he had kept the faith and loved the Lord's soon appearing (2 Timothy 4:7–8). ❋

December 10

There was a man in Jerusalem, whose name was Simeon; and the same man was just and devout, waiting for the consolation of Israel: and the Holy Ghost was upon him. And it was revealed unto him by the Holy Ghost, that he should not see death, before he had seen the Lord's Christ. And he came by the Spirit into the temple: and when the parents brought in the child Jesus, to do for him after the custom of the law, Then took he him up in his arms, and blessed God, and said, Lord, now lettest thou thy servant depart in peace, according to thy word: For mine eyes have seen thy salvation, Which thou hast prepared before the face of all people; A light to lighten the Gentiles, and the glory of thy people Israel. And Joseph and his mother marvelled at those things which were spoken of him. And Simeon blessed them, and said unto Mary his mother, Behold, this child is set for the fall and rising again of many in Israel; and for a sign which shall be spoken against; (Yea, a sword shall pierce through thy own soul also,) that the thoughts of many hearts may be revealed.

LUKE 2:25–35

MORNING

Each person who described Jesus near the time of His birth saw Him as something different. Elizabeth, the mother of John the Baptist called Jesus "my Lord" (Luke 1:43). Her husband Zechariah, in a rich prophetic vision, called Jesus a "horn of salvation" and the "dayspring from on high" (Luke 1:69, 78). And don't forget Mary, the young mother, who called her child God's gift of help to Israel (Luke 1:54).

The angel told the shepherds that the babe in the manger was the Savior of Israel (Luke 2:8–12). The wise men knew Jesus as the King of the Jews (Matthew 2:2). Herod saw Jesus as a political rival and so tried to destroy Him (Matthew 2:16–18). The old prophetess Anna saw in Jesus the redemption of Jerusalem (Luke 2:36–38).

This is the child of Christmas. He is the Lord, the Dayspring from on High, and God's gift of help to Israel. Not only so, He is Israel's Savior and Messiah, the King of the Jews, the rival to all kings, and the redemption of Jerusalem.

Simeon, however, saw more in this divine baby boy than anyone else: He was not only God's gift to Israel, but a blessing to the whole world. Simeon understood what the others did not; that Christ was "prepared before the face of all people" (Luke 2:31). In other words, Jesus was not to be hidden in this distant province of the Roman Empire. He was not just the glory of Israel, but also a light to enlighten the Gentiles (Luke 2:32). Simeon knew the prophecies of Isaiah concerning the promised Messiah: "It is a light thing that thou shouldest be my servant to raise up the tribes of Jacob, and to restore the preserved of Israel: I will also give thee for a light to the Gentiles, that thou mayest be my salvation unto the end of the earth" (Isaiah 49:6).

And so, when Jesus came out of the wilderness to begin His ministry, "He came and dwelt in Capernaum, which is upon the sea coast, in the borders of Zabulon and Nephthalim: That it might be fulfilled which was spoken by Esaias the prophet, saying, The land of Zabulon, and the land of Nephthalim, by the way of the sea, beyond Jordan, Galilee of the Gentiles; The people which sat in darkness saw great light; and to them which sat in the region and shadow of death light is sprung up" (Matthew 4:13–16).

Night

Simeon told Mary and Joseph that the baby Jesus was the glory of God's people, Israel (Luke 2:32). It was an honor to the Jewish nation that the Messiah had come out of one of their tribes and would live and soon die among them. This glory will be theirs always. "No longer will you need the sun. . .nor the moon to give its light. . .," declared Isaiah, "for the LORD your God will be your everlasting light, and your God will be your glory" (Isaiah 60:19 NLT).

No wonder Joseph and Mary marveled at the things Simeon said about this boy. If that had been my baby, I would have been full of pride— "My child is the light of the Gentiles and the glory of Israel!"

But Simeon had more to say, which would temper whatever joy the child's parents may have felt, for he foretold Jesus' death some thirty years later saying, "Behold, this child is set for the fall and rising again of many in Israel; and for a sign which shall be spoken against. . . that the thoughts of many hearts may be revealed" (Luke 2:34–35). With these words Simeon again drew from Isaiah to describe the child.

Isaiah had said, "He shall be for a sanctuary; but for a stone of stumbling and for a rock of offence to both the houses of Israel, for a gin and for a snare to the inhabitants of Jerusalem. And many among them shall stumble, and fall, and be broken" (8:14–15). Does this sound like the Jesus people talk about at Christmas? It is none other than He. Jesus Christ was the stumbling stone for the Jews (1 Peter 2:8). Gentiles, on the other hand, experienced Christ as a stepping-stone up out of darkness into God's light (Ephesians 3:2–6).

Unlike the others, Simeon predicted the infant's death: "Yea, a sword shall pierce through thy own soul also," he said (Luke 2:35). This prophecy of suffering and death and stumbling and eventual glory was spoken at Jesus' circumcision ceremony when the child was only eight days old—and began to be fulfilled some thirty years later as Mary stood by watching Jesus be crucified. ❋

December 11

And there was one Anna, a prophetess,
the daughter of Phanuel, of the tribe of
Aser: she was of a great age, and had lived
with an husband seven years from her
virginity; And she was a widow of about
fourscore and four years, which departed
not from the temple, but served God with
fastings and prayers night and day. And
she coming in that instant gave thanks
likewise unto the Lord, and spake
of him to all them that looked for
redemption in Jerusalem.

LUKE 2:36–38

Morning

Consider the scene at the Temple in Jerusalem. The "Word made flesh" is held in young Mary's arms awaiting His circumcision. He who could claim equality with God has made Himself nothing (Philippians 2:6–7). He and Mary are anonymous among a crowd of other newborns and mothers there for the same reason.

Joseph is there as well, holding two pigeons, the offering required by the Law for this ceremony. Yet he knows that the baby in his wife's embrace will be called Immanuel, which means *God with us* (Matthew 1:23). The Temple designed for the worship of this same God surrounds the little family.

There the Christ-child is honored despite His anonymity. Two people acknowledge Him. One is Simeon, who actually holds the baby in his arms. "Lord, now let your servant die in peace," he prays. "I have seen your salvation" (Luke 2:29–30 NLT). Then he tells of the child's life and purpose: He will be the glory of Israel, the light of the Gentiles, and the cause of the falling and rising of many people. His mother's heart will break while her son is crucified as a sign from God that will be spoken against (Luke 2:32–35).

A woman also bears testimony in this new beginning. She is the aged widow Anna, a prophetess constantly at prayer in the Temple. Anna saw the baby, knew who He was, and did two things that we should find helpful.

First, Anna thanked God (Luke 2:38). A little thankfulness for the birth of Christ is a strong antidote to the excesses of the Christmas season. Try this in the mall, at the ATM, or when you've had too much fudge. Say a little prayer like Anna's: "Thank You, dear

Father, that my eyes have seen Your salvation!"

Second, Anna spoke about the Christ-child to everyone who was looking for the redemption of Israel. This we can do as well. From time to time, as Christmas approaches, gently remind others that "unto you is born this day in the city of David a Saviour, which is Christ the Lord" (Luke 2:11).

Night

Anna was always at the Temple serving God with fasting and prayer, night and day. Have you noticed there are often women like Anna around, who are devout, with a mind to serve God, yet little known?

Long ago, when Moses was building the tabernacle, there were women who served at the door of that highly crafted tent (Exodus 38:8). Maybe we can understand Anna better by considering these women; it may also help us in finding Christ in Christmas.

Nothing much is said about the women in Exodus, but we do know that they gave up their mirrors to be used in fabricating the brass laver. Such mirrors were made of fine brass, highly polished, just the right material for the laver, which was a large bowl filled with water and set in a brass base. The priests used the laver to wash their hands and feet before they offered the sacrifices (Exodus 30:18–20).

It is unknown how many ministering women gave their mirrors for the laver, but there must have been a good number of them because their mirrors were small and the laver was big. These ancient women had somehow overcome their self-love. They no longer gazed at themselves in mirrors. They gave their mirrors up to make the worship of God possible, for without washing in the laver, the priests could not offer sacrifices (Exodus 30:21). In the same way, it is impossible to love the Lord if one gazes at oneself in the mirror of this world. This is why, among all those who crowded the Temple that day, Anna recognized Christ. She spent her life looking to God, not herself, and thus able to recognize the Savior.

A story in Luke 7:36–50 illustrates this: A

Pharisee invited Jesus to supper, though he was blind to the true identity of the Savior. He didn't offer water for foot washing, there was no kiss of greeting, or an anointing of olive oil. This Pharisee was gazing at himself in a metaphorical brass mirror and so could not serve the Lord.

In contrast, a certain immoral woman heard Jesus was at that Pharisee's house. She went there carrying a beautiful jar filled with expensive perfume, knelt, and wept. Her tears fell on Jesus' feet and she wiped them off with her hair, her own glory (1 Corinthians 11:15), to wipe the dust off Jesus' feet. She had no mirror, no self-glory. ❅

December 12

These things write I unto thee, hoping to
come unto thee shortly: But if I tarry long,
that thou mayest know how thou oughtest
to behave thyself in the house of God,
which is the church of the living God,
the pillar and ground of the truth. And
without controversy great is the mystery
of godliness: God was manifest in the
flesh, justified in the Spirit, seen of angels,
preached unto the Gentiles, believed on
in the world, received up into glory.

1 TIMOTHY 3:14–16

Morning

Last Christmas I saw a bumper sticker that said, Keep the X in Xmas, mocking the saying, "Keep Christ in Christmas." American Puritans, who tried to outlaw Christmas in the American colonies, may have liked the word *Xmas* because for them Christ never was in Christmas.

During the past 120 years, Christmas has developed into a holiday of overabundance rather than a season to remember the birth of the Savior. Previously it was more religious, a season carefully observed in liturgical worship by Episcopal and Lutheran churches. Christians did, and still do, celebrate the birth of Christ, but this is snowed under by the secular holiday. Can anyone get Christ back in Christmas?

When the apostle Paul wrote to Timothy, he

was concerned that people know how to live as Christians—how to live in the house of God, the church. The metaphor he used to describe the church explains not how to keep Christ in Christmas, but how we might keep Christ in the church—an even more important endeavor, I'd say.

Paul called the church "the pillar and ground of the truth" (1 Timothy 3:15) In other words, in this world, the church is the sole support of the truth. So let's ask Paul, "What is the truth?" His answer is, "Great is the mystery of godliness" (1 Timothy 3:16).

The Christian faith is a collection of mysteries that cannot be found out through reasoning because they are *above* reason. They are not mysteries of philosophy or speculation or science, far surpassing all these. Not only so, they are revealed mysteries, no longer hidden or sealed. So elsewhere Paul wrote of his desire "to make all men see what is the fellowship of the mystery, which from the beginning of the world hath been hid in God" (Ephesians 3:9).

These revealed mysteries are the wonder of Christmas because they all reveal Christ. The apostle Paul was a minister of "the mystery which hath been hid from ages and from generations, but now is made manifest to his saints" (Colossians 1:26). Those who wish to keep Christ in this season and every season, indeed every day of the year, can recall "what is the riches of the glory of this mystery among the Gentiles; which is Christ in you, the hope of glory" (Colossians 1:27).

NIGHT

Though not a Christmas song, William Cowper's "God Moves in a Mysterious Way" is well loved among believers, and its title at least is familiar to people who may have never sung a hymn. Its first lines read:

God moves in a mysterious way
His wonders to perform;
He plants His footsteps in the sea,
And rides upon the storm.

The mysterious ways of God began to be much less mysterious when Jesus Christ was born at Bethlehem. God is an invisible Spirit (John 4:24; 1 Timothy 6:16). Yet the Son of God is the visible, tangible embodiment of the invisible God (Colossians 1:15). That is why a believer's heart thrills at these words: "The Word was made flesh, and dwelt among us. . .full of grace and truth" (John 1:14). That Word is the message that explains God.

Only in the Son can God be seen and understood, therefore the disciples were exposed to God's attributes in Jesus Christ (John 14:9–10). Even more so, God is understood through the revelation of Christ in the scriptures and nowhere else. All images such as statues and pictures that pretend to portray God are condemned in scripture (Deuteronomy 5:8). They exchange "the glory of the immortal God for images resembling a mortal human being or birds or four-footed animals or reptiles" (Romans 1:23 NRSV).

Why is God so opposed to these idols? Because they are caricatures that misrepresent and dishonor Him. In some cases, idols may suggest a few of God's attributes. Yet these are partial and distorted. He is jealous of them because they divert our love away from Him (Deuteronomy 5:8–9). Also, idols lack essential life, love, and light. Only the living, loving, enlightening image of the invisible God revealed in scripture can bring the divine essence and attributes to us (Colossians 1:13–15).

Here is what we can see there: Long before Jesus lived in Galilee, God created everything in the Son (Colossians 1:16). The celestial and terrestrial spheres and every form of power and authority exist through Him and for Him. In addition to this, all things are held together in Him for the accomplishment of God's purpose (Colossians 1:17). All this was formerly a mystery, but since Jesus Christ was born and the apostle Paul completed the Word of God (Colossians 1:25), that mystery is revealed and we know that God exclusively operates, is seen, and is understood through Christ. ✳

December 13

But thou, Bethlehem Ephratah, though
thou be little among the thousands of
Judah, yet out of thee shall he come forth
unto me that is to be ruler in Israel;
whose goings forth have been from of old,
from everlasting. Therefore will he give
them up, until the time that she which
travaileth hath brought forth: then the
remnant of his brethren shall return unto
the children of Israel. And he shall stand
and feed in the strength of the LORD, in the
majesty of the name of the LORD his God;
and they shall abide: for now shall he
be great unto the ends of the earth.
And this man shall be the peace.

MICAH 5:2–5

MORNING

When the wise men arrived in Jerusalem, they asked, "Where is he that is born King of the Jews? for we have seen his star in the east, and are come to worship him" (Matthew 2:2). The scribes paraphrased Micah 5:2 with great assurance: "And thou Bethlehem, land of Judah, Art in no wise least among the princes of Judah: For out of thee shall come forth a governor, Who shall be shepherd of my people Israel" (Matthew 2:6 ASV). It seemed to be well known among the Jews that Christ should come out of the town of Bethlehem where David lived (John 7:42).

Why do you think little Bethlehem should be the place of Christ's nativity? It is significant for at least two reasons. The first reason is bread. In the prophecy of Micah, Christ is standing and feeding the flock "in the strength of the LORD, in the majesty of the name of the LORD his God" (5:4). In Bethlehem, which means *the house of bread*, Jesus came down from heaven (John 6:51) to feed the human race with the bread of life.

Christ still stands today, feeding us Himself, the bread of heaven. "Whoever eats my flesh and drinks my blood remains in me, and I in them," says Jesus. "Just as the living Father sent me and I live because of the Father, so the one who feeds on me will live because of me. This is the bread that came down from heaven" (John 6:55–58 NIV).

The second reason is the shepherd. The night of Christ's birth, shepherds heard this good news: "For unto you is born this day in the city of David a Saviour, which is Christ the Lord" (Luke 2:11). They hurried to Bethlehem when they heard this news. Bethlehem was called the city of David because it was formerly the home of David, who began as a shepherd and later became king of Israel (1 Samuel 16:1, 11–13). The night of Jesus' birth, those shepherds greeted the birth of another shepherd (Matthew 2:6), "that great shepherd of the sheep" (Hebrews 13:20) who called himself "the good shepherd" (John 10:11). They found their Shepherd in Bethlehem as promised, but ironically lying in a manger, a feed trough for sheep and other livestock.

NIGHT

An angel told the shepherds to find the newborn Christ in the city of David, that is, Bethlehem. Jesus was born in this, the former home of David, king of Israel, because He is the ruler of the kingdom of God, the continuation of David's kingdom. This is an important part of the Christmas story. As Gabriel told Mary: "The Lord God shall give unto him the throne of his father David: And he shall reign over the house of Jacob for ever; and of his kingdom there shall be no end" (Luke 1:32–33).

When Jesus was born, the royal line of David had been deposed from its throne for half a millennium. Yet God promised many times that David's kingdom would never end. For example, God promised Solomon, "I will establish the throne of thy kingdom upon Israel for ever, as

I promised to David thy father" (1 Kings 9:5). Christ's birth fulfilled this promise.

Yet, on the hill of Calvary the disciples of Jesus Christ heard their dying master cry, "My God, my God, why hast thou forsaken me?" (Mark 15:34). How could this fulfill the promise of the kingdom? Hadn't He once said, "He that sent me is with me: the Father hath not left me alone" (John 8:29)?

Things did not turn out as expected. The man they thought was Israel's Messiah had, it seemed, given up in despair. The men and women who followed Jesus through Galilee were faithful, but they didn't know that it is not His birth, not His life, but His death that is at the heart of everything that will occur until the completion of the ages.

The declaration that "The kingdoms of this world are become the kingdoms of our Lord, and of his Christ" is a major milestone along that way (Revelation 11:15). It is the beginning of the thousand-year kingdom (Revelation 20:4–7). After this, the heavens will pass away with a great noise, the elements will melt with fervent heat, and the earth will burn up (2 Peter 3:10). This cataclysm, like the deluge in Noah's day, clears the way for a fresh start. It is the beginning of a new creation in which the Lamb that the disciples saw sacrificed will reign until the last enemy—death—is abolished (Revelation 20:11; 21:1; 22:3; 1 Corinthians 15:23–28).

This, the destruction of death, is the finish that was declared by the Son of Man as He died on the cross; His enemies are subdued, and the kingdom becomes the Father's. Let's all mark this in our Bible as the consummation of the ages when God at last becomes "all in all" (1 Corinthians 15:28). ❋

December 14

*For unto us a child is born, unto us a son
is given: and the government shall be
upon his shoulder: and his name shall be
called Wonderful, Counsellor, The mighty
God, The everlasting Father, The
Prince of Peace.*

Isaiah 9:6

MORNING

Isaiah's inspiration draws together into one sentence the human and divine natures of our Savior. "For unto us a *child* is born, unto us a *son* is given" (Isaiah 9:6, emphasis added). Jesus Christ was a child in His human nature, and so He was *born*—a child like any other that ever lived upon the face of the earth.

But Jesus Christ was not only born to us as the Son of Man. He is given to us as the Son of God. Isaiah said that Christ the Son who was in the beginning with God (John 1:1–2), was *given* to us. This truth is deep and difficult to express, yet it is the wonder of Christmas. The human and divine have come together in Christ. This is why He can be the mediator of God and man (1 Timothy 2:5). He knows both sides, He can speak for both, and can reconcile the world to God (2 Corinthians 5:18–19). He is the complete ransom payment.

What was the value of the ransom payment Christ made? Scripture accounts for two amounts: the Son of Man gave His soul a ransom for many, and the Mediator gave Himself a ransom for all (Matthew 20:28; 1 Timothy 2:5–6).

A person's soul is the record and expression of his life experience. So the ransom of the Son of Man's soul recalls that Jesus Christ, born of a woman, came to serve, not to be served. Though He was rich, for our sake He became poor. He was in the form of God, yet emptied Himself, assumed a human form, and descended to the death of the cross. He knew no sin, yet was made sin for us. These experiences composed the soul that He poured out in death (Mark 14:34), which is the price He paid for the ransom of many.

Furthermore, since Matthew wrote to

Jewish believers describing Jesus Christ as Israel's king, the "many" here refers to the citizens of Israel (Matthew 20:28). But God is more than the God of many Jews; He is the God of all creation. Therefore, the exalted Christ is the Mediator with God who not only gave His soul for many, but Himself as the ransom for all.

NIGHT

Scripture describes how the immeasurable value of Christ's suffering and shame was amplified by the glory and power of His resurrection and ascension. When lowered to the poverty of the cross, he ransomed the many. Now, He is no longer poor but is the exalted embodiment of infinite wealth at the right hand of God. There, the Mediator is able to satisfy God as the ransom for all.

This all began with the Christmas story found in the Gospels and is expanded and completed in the epistles. It is the story of Christ Jesus who was in the form of God, yet took the form of a slave and descended to the curse of the cross, voluntarily sinking from the highest to the lowest place in the universe. *Jesus* is the Son of God's name in that humiliation.

His exaltation reverses this humiliating journey until every tongue has declared that Jesus is Lord for the glory of God the Father (Philippians 2:5–11). Then, when all is subjected to Him at the end of the ages, the One who was the lowest shall be universally acknowledged as the highest, God's plan will be complete, and God will be all in all (1 Corinthians 15:28).

Since the day of Christ's resurrection, God has been engaged in the exaltation of the Son. Many celestial powers now submit to our Lord (1 Peter 3:22), and when He returns, the entire earth will be added to His sphere of influence. Finally, because of His utter humiliation and death on the cross, the whole universe will be reconciled to God (Colossians 1:20). "Who, being in the form of God, thought it not robbery to be equal with God: But made himself of no reputation, and took upon him the form of a servant, and was made in the likeness of men: And being found in fashion as a man, he humbled himself, and became obedient unto death, even the death of the cross" (Philippians 2:6–8). ✽

December 15

And the Word was made flesh, and dwelt among us, (and we beheld his glory, the glory as of the only begotten of the Father,) full of grace and truth. John bare witness of him, and cried, saying, This was he of whom I spake, He that cometh after me is preferred before me: for he was before me. And of his fulness have all we received, and grace for grace. For the law was given by Moses, but grace and truth came by Jesus Christ. No man hath seen God at any time, the only begotten Son, which is in the bosom of the Father, he hath declared him.

JOHN 1:14–18

Morning

Jesus Christ's birth is called the *Incarnation*. It marked a sea of change in human history. There was never anyone like this man. Though He had mind and body, and experienced joy and suffering like us (yet without sin), He was entirely God. This is such a mystery that even the inspired words of the Bible struggle to express it. Sometimes it seems even the scriptures resort to literary devices like metaphor and analogy to help us understand the mystery of God. For example:

One day, an old man named Abraham and his son, Isaac, trekked up a mountain called Moriah. Abraham carried a knife and hot coals for a fire. Isaac carried firewood. When they stopped to rest, Isaac said, "Father?"

"Yes, my son."

"We have the wood and the fire, but where is the lamb for the sacrifice?"

Abraham answered, "My son, the Lord will provide a lamb" (see Genesis 22:3–8).

Three days before, God had told Abraham, "Take your son, your only son—yes, Isaac, whom you love so much—and go to the land of Moriah. Go and sacrifice him as a burnt offering on one of the mountains, which I will show you" (Genesis 22:2 NLT). So Abraham, the father of faith, set off to do just this.

The end of this story reveals God in incarnation. Meanwhile let's look at how it reveals Abraham's faith, which carried the human race to the day of Christ's birth.

On a certain night before the birth of Isaac, God took Abraham outside and said, "Look up at the sky and count the stars—if indeed you can count them. . . . So shall your offspring be" (Genesis 15:5 NIV). That night Abraham "believed the LORD, and he credited it to him as righteousness" (Genesis 15:6 NIV). That night marked the beginning of faith in God's promises. But what if Abraham had killed Isaac? Then he wouldn't have had even one son, much less numberless offspring like the stars in the sky. If Isaac were dead, God's promise, given on that starry night, would be nullified. But Abraham believed, and continued to believe.

Now, picture Abraham and Isaac trudging up that slope. Isaac asks, "We have the wood and the fire, but where is the lamb for the sacrifice?"

The faithful old man answers, "My son, the Lord will provide a lamb." This story and this statement of faith describe the journey and hope of Israel, which reached its apex the day Gabriel told Mary, "And, behold, thou shalt conceive in thy womb, and bring forth a son, and shalt call his name JESUS. He shall be great,

and shall be called the Son of the Highest: and
the Lord God shall give unto him the throne
of his father David: And he shall reign over the
house of Jacob for ever; and of his kingdom
there shall be no end" (Luke 1:31–33).

NIGHT

When Abraham and Isaac arrived at the mountaintop, Abraham built an altar and placed the wood on it. Then he bound Isaac and laid him on the altar over the wood. Abraham held the knife and lifted it to kill his son as a sacrifice to the Lord. In his heart he believed, *God will provide a lamb.* Suddenly the angel of the Lord called out of heaven, "Abraham, Abraham!"

The old believer calmly said, "Here I am."

"Lay down the knife," said the angel. "Do not hurt the boy, for now I know that you truly reverence God. You have not even held back your beloved son from me."

Abraham looked up from the altar where his son lay, and there, entangled by the horns in a thicket of brush, was a ram. This

ram became the sacrifice in place of Isaac
(see Genesis 22:9–13).

The ram was strong and powerful, but the
instruments of his power, his horns, were
caught in a thicket. This rendered him helpless,
easily caught and sacrificed.

Isn't this ram like Christ? "Who, being in the
form of God, thought it not robbery to be equal
with God: But made himself of no reputation,
and took upon him the form of a servant, and
was made in the likeness of men: And being
found in fashion as a man, he humbled himself,
and became obedient unto death, even the
death of the cross" (Philippians 2:6–8).

In the act of incarnation—of becoming the
man Jesus—God's Son became thoroughly
entangled in the complex thicket of human
existence. He was first a helpless baby, then
a child. Finally, when Jesus was "grown, he
seemed to be as ordinary as the next man"

(Matthew 13:55). Few people, if any, could see that in this man, God had provided a Lamb.

After His work on earth was complete, people brought the good news of Jesus into the world, and here is what they discovered: "For the Jews require a sign, and the Greeks seek after wisdom: But we preach Christ crucified, unto the Jews a stumblingblock, and unto the Greeks foolishness; But unto them which are called, both Jews and Greeks, Christ the power of God, and the wisdom of God. Because the foolishness of God is wiser than men; and the weakness of God is stronger than men (1 Corinthians 1:22–25). ❄

December 16

God, who at sundry times and in divers
manners spake in time past unto the fathers
by the prophets, Hath in these last days spoken unto
us by his Son, whom he hath appointed heir of all
things, by whom also he made the worlds; Who being
the brightness of his glory, and the express image
of his person, and upholding all things by the word
of his power, when he had by himself purged our sins,
sat down on the right hand of the Majesty on high:
Being made so much better than the angels, as he hath
by inheritance obtained a more excellent name than
they. For unto which of the angels said he at any time,
Thou art my Son, this day have I begotten thee?
And again, I will be to him a Father, and he shall be
to me a Son? And again, when he bringeth in the
firstbegotten into the world, he saith, And let all the
angels of God worship him.

Hebrews 1:1–6

MORNING

What are we celebrating at Christmastime? Everyone must know. Somewhere under layers of entertainment and buying and selling and eating and drinking and dressing and decorating is an extraordinary child who rested in a manger.

Long ago Christians began to use this season as a time to remember that "when the fulness of the time was come, God sent forth his Son, made of a woman" (Galatians 4:4). But what does this mean? The above verses from the book of Galatians explain it: When that baby was born, the way that God relates to humanity forever changed.

Before the nativity of Jesus, God spoke many times and in many ways through the Israel's prophets. What was the message they spoke? To

Adam, it was that Christ would come from the seed of the woman (Genesis 3:15); to Abraham, that Christ would be his descendant (Genesis 22:18); to Jacob, that Christ would spring from the tribe of Judah (Genesis 49:8); to David, that Christ would be of his household (2 Samuel 7:16); to Micah, that Christ would be born at Bethlehem (Micah 5:2); to Isaiah, that Christ would be born of a virgin (Isaiah 7:14).

Hebrews 1:1 does not say that in the past God spoke at many times and in various ways about many things. No, God spoke about one thing—Christ. The Bible is about Christ, and those who see this have found a key to understanding it.

The days are past when the divine speaking was *about* Christ. In these last days God has spoken unto us *by* and *in* the Son. The babe in the manger is the speaking of God. He is also the message.

Hebrews calls these the last days because

God's speaking in Christ is the final revelation. At first there was the revelation of God through the creation (Romans 1:20). Then came the dreams, visions, and voices seen and heard by the patriarchs (Genesis 12:1). Next came the Mosaic revelation in the law (Exodus 20:1–18). At last, the prophets explained the law and revealed more of the coming Christ (Isaiah 9:6–7).

Then the fullness of time came and God sent the Son, made of a woman (Galatians 4:4). He is the final revelation of God to us. In these days we enjoy the promised Spirit of truth who abides with us and lives in us to teach us all that Christ was and is and will be (John 14:16–17, 26).

NIGHT

At the birth of Jesus "a great company of the heavenly host appeared. . .praising God and saying, 'Glory to God in the highest heaven, and on earth peace to those on whom his favor rests'" (Luke 2:13–14 NIV). I like the last words of this angelic praise—"peace to those on whom his favor rests." God had not come to angels or any other creature, but had favored humanity by sending His son.

The ancient prophets wanted to know about this. They foretold what God had prepared for us, even though they had questions about what it could mean. The Spirit of Christ within told them in advance about the Son's suffering and His glory afterward. They wondered at this and wanted to know when and to whom it would happen. They were told that these things would not happen during their lifetime, but years later. Even the angels "long to look into these things" (1 Peter 1:10–12).

Images of angels are favorites during Christmas. They appear as tree ornaments and house decorations. The real angels desire to know all about the person and work of the Son of God. But God's favor rests not on them; rather, God's favor rests on you and me. It is *our* privilege, among all creation, to know the Son of God.

Hebrews chapter one helps us better know the Son. First, before anything was made, God promised all to the Son as an inheritance. Then through the Son, God made the universe and everything in it (Hebrews 1:2). Throughout creation, the Son reflects God's glory and represents God exactly. As if this were not enough, the Son also sustains the universe by the power of His word. After He died, solving the problem of sin, He sat down in honor at the right hand of God's heavenly majesty (Hebrews 1:3).

This brings us up to date in the progress of God's beloved Son. The remainder of Hebrews 1 reveals more of Christ until a future day when He will roll up the old creation like clothing. By that time, it will have perished, but He remains forever until His enemies have become a footstool under His feet (Hebrews 1:10–13). Then at last God will be all in all (1 Corinthians 15:28). ❋

December 17

In the beginning was the Word, and the
Word was with God, and the Word was God.

JOHN 1:1

Behold, a virgin shall be with child, and
shall bring forth a son, and they shall
call his name Emmanuel, which being
interpreted is, God with us.

MATTHEW 1:23

And, behold, thou shalt conceive in thy
womb, and bring forth a son, and shalt
call his name JESUS.

LUKE 1:31

Morning

Recently I was asked for my Social Security card, but I hadn't seen it for years. So I went to the Social Security office to get another one. Naturally, they needed proof that I am who I am. This was a problem because I had no valid identification showing my complete name. I've never used my complete name. With some effort, I eventually solved the problem, and now I have a little blue and white numbered card to prove what is my name. You can be sure I'm much more careful about my name now!

Your name is a type of shorthand for who you are and what you have done. For example, when you hear the name Abraham Lincoln, you think of the man who emerged from the American wilderness to become president and whose actions saved the Union. If you know the name Emily Dickinson, you think of a reclusive woman in a small New England town who wrote some of the finest poetry in the English language.

In the beginning, the Word was with God (John 1:1), and John was somehow inspired to write about Him. But John was slow to tell us the name of the One who is the Word. Suppose you were the first to read John's manuscript. Imagine your desire to find out who is the Word? You'd say, "He must have a name! I must find Him!"

As you read John's Gospel, the apostle leads you from the beginning before all beginnings, tracking the Word—through whom all things were made, who is the life that is the light of men—all the way through rejection and acceptance. Yet he gives the Word no other name. You read on and see that the Word became flesh with the glory of the only begotten of the Father. Ah! He is now flesh. You're getting close! Without doubt He was given a name. "Who is this one who is full of grace and truth," you ask; "whose fullness we have all received, even grace upon grace?" (see John 1:2–16).

Suddenly, in verse 17 you are told something you already know: "The law was given by Moses." Of course it was. Is nothing new? "But grace and truth *[grace and truth!]* came through Jesus Christ." Finally. You have found the name above all names. It is Jesus Christ. He is the Word who was with God and is speaking from God to you, and to God for you (Hebrews 1:2; 1 Timothy 2:5).

NIGHT

An angel made sure that Mary and Joseph knew that the holy child to be born of Mary had a name. He told Joseph that the child would be known as Immanuel, meaning, *God with us.* He told Mary to name the child Jesus, meaning, *God is salvation* (Matthew 1:23; Luke 1:31).

Pity the people who use the name Jesus Christ as a curse—for them it has no meaning or power. When you hear someone use the Lord's name like this, pray for that person who does not know the marvel of it.

What does this name mean? It means that here is someone who, though He could claim equality with God, did not cling to that privilege. He made himself nothing; He took the form of a slave, came in the likeness of humanity, and humbled Himself even further by dying a criminal's death on a cross (Philippians 2:6–8). That death reconciled the entire creation to God. And because He was resurrected from the dead, death was stripped of its power. Though many people have been presidents and many have been poets, not one has been or ever again will be what Jesus Christ is (see Colossians 1:14–20).

Because of this, God raised Jesus to the heights of heaven and gave Him a name that is above every other name, so that at the name of Jesus every knee will surely bow, in heaven and on earth and under the earth, and every tongue will confess that Jesus Christ is Lord, and their confession will glorify God the Father (Philippians 2:9–11).

The word *Jesus* on the lips of a believer has power that cannot be exaggerated. Long ago some Christians were told, "Do you not know that wrongdoers will not inherit the kingdom of God? Do not be deceived: Neither the sexually immoral nor idolaters, nor adulterers nor male prostitutes nor homosexual offenders nor thieves nor the greedy nor drunkards nor slanderers nor swindlers will inherit the kingdom of God (1 Corinthians 6:9–10 NIV). Then they were bluntly informed, "That is what some of you were. *But* you were washed, you were sanctified, you were justified *in the name of the Lord Jesus Christ* and by the Spirit of our God" (1 Corinthians 6:11, emphasis added). ❄

December 18

And the angel said unto them, Fear not:
for, behold, I bring you good tidings of
great joy, which shall be to all people.
For unto you is born this day in the city
of David a Saviour, which is Christ the
Lord. And this shall be a sign unto you; Ye
shall find the babe wrapped in swaddling
clothes, lying in a manger. And suddenly
there was with the angel a multitude of the
heavenly host praising God, and saying,
Glory to God in the highest, and on earth
peace, good will toward men.

LUKE 2:10–14

MORNING

How many times have angels sung God's praises? Scripture says they were present at the creation when "the morning stars sang together, and all the sons of God shouted for joy" (Job 38:7). At the end of time they'll be found chanting, "Blessing, and glory, and wisdom, and thanksgiving, and honour, and power, and might, be unto our God for ever and ever" (Revelation 7:12).

But when the angels saw that God had become a suckling infant upon a woman's breast, they reached for even higher notes. Singing "Glory to God in the highest" (Luke 2:14), the angel choir gave the most soaring praise for the most amazing accomplishment of all time.

The Scots hymn writer James Montgomery (1771–1854) wrote about a call that went out among the angels, summoning them to that field near Bethlehem:

Angels, from the realms of glory,
Wing your downward flight to earth,
Ye who sing creation's story,
Now proclaim Messiah's birth.

I can just imagine how those multitudes of angels rushed to that place to sing "Glory to God in the highest" and add a wonderfully new phrase to the lexicon of faith: "And on earth peace, good will toward men" (Luke 2:14). Since the day Adam and Eve were sent out from the garden, there had been no peace on earth, especially not in the human heart. But when that child was born, when that Son was given whose name is "The Prince of Peace" (Isaiah 9:6), those angels sang a new song, which is our gospel: "On earth peace, good will toward men."

Some people picture God angrily throwing lightning bolts from His throne in heaven. Others see a cold, distant, uncaring God. But this is not who is revealed in the Bible. Can there be greater proof of God's loving-kindness toward us than the gift of His beloved Son, the Prince of Peace?

Look around you, at all the people bustling about on their Christmastime errands. Remember that God's good will has not come only to a select few, but to all humanity—even to those who curse God, who sin grievously against Him, or who simply have not yet heard the gracious invitation: "Come now, and let us reason together. . .though your sins be as scarlet, they shall be as white as snow; though they be red like crimson, they shall be as wool" (Isaiah 1:18).

NIGHT

Not only angels give glory to God. There is divine glory in every dewdrop that twinkles in the morning sun. That glory is magnified in every warbling bird. The entire creation is an instrument of God's praise. That's why the scripture declares, "Let the heavens rejoice, and let the earth be glad; let the sea roar, and the fulness thereof. Let the field be joyful, and all that is therein: then shall all the trees of the wood rejoice Before the Lord" (Psalm 96:11–13).

But creation, as unfathomable as it is, cannot sing a song as sweet and meaningful as that of the birth of Jesus Christ. There is more melody in the baby Jesus lying in the manger than in all the galaxies that roll through God's unending universe. That child is the Son of God. In Him God's love came into the creation (John 3:16).

Before Christ came, the creation revealed "God's invisible qualities—his eternal power and divine nature" (Romans 1:20 NIV). If people ignore or deny God's existence, the testimony of creation gives them no excuse to do so. Yet the creation only expresses the Creator. In Christ, God is entirely and personally seen. He is "the radiance of God's glory and the exact representation of his being" (Hebrews 1:3 NIV).

The Son bears the true character of the Father, having the same image and likeness. In the power, wisdom, and goodness of Jesus Christ, we see the power, wisdom, and goodness of the invisible God. That's why Jesus had the following conversation with one of His disciples: "If you really know me, you will know my Father as well. From now on, you do know him and have seen him." Philip said, "Lord, show us the Father and that will be enough for us." Jesus answered: "Don't you know me, Philip, even after I have been among you such a long time? Anyone who has seen me has seen the Father. How can you say, 'Show us the Father'? (John 14:7–9 NIV).

No wonder the multitude of the heavenly host praised God on the birthday of Jesus Christ! They understood the true wonder of Christmas: that in Jesus Christ dwells "all the fulness of the Godhead bodily" (Colossians 2:9). ❇

December 19

For it is not possible that the blood of bulls and of goats should take away sins. Wherefore when he cometh into the world, he saith, Sacrifice and offering thou wouldest not, but a body hast thou prepared me: In burnt offerings and sacrifices for sin thou hast had no pleasure. Then said I, Lo, I come (in the volume of the book it is written of me,) to do thy will, O God.

Hebrews 10:4–7

MORNING

You might say, "I thought this was a book about Christmas. Why am I reading verses about the blood of bulls and goats, burnt offerings, and sacrifices for sin?" True, there is no tinsel and lights and artificial snow in these words. But I think one must get through such pretty things—open them like wrapping paper and ribbon to get at the gift of Christmas. Real joy can be found in Christmas when one drops the last syllable of the word—*mas*—and finds Christ.

These verses show the glory of Christmas without the—*mas*: "Sacrifice and offering you did not desire, but a body you prepared for me. . . . I said, 'Here I am—it is written about me in the scroll—I have come to do your will, O God'" (Hebrews 10:5–7 NIV).

The days depicted in the Old Testament were full of animal sacrifices. These were ordained in the Law of Moses because the blood of bulls and goats atoned for sin. However, as mentioned earlier in Hebrews 10, these sacrifices were only a shadow of things to come (verse 1). The person casting that shadow was Christ. He is the real sacrifice for sin. The shadow-sacrifices, the bulls and goats, were only meant to indicate that Christ would indeed come.

Those shadowy sacrifices were repeated again and again, year after year, but they never solved the problem of sin for those who came to worship. If they had, the sacrifices would have stopped; the worshippers would have been purified from sin forever. This is explained in Hebrews 10:1–4.

Now, after the birth, death, burial, and resurrection of Christ, good things have come. The redemption is perfect, never to be repeated.

You and I and all believers have complete justification from sin (Romans 5:8–9). The death of Christ satisfied God's justice so believers freely receive the abundance of grace and the gift of righteousness (Romans 5:17). Scripture repeatedly states that when Christ died we died with Him. This is seen most famously in Galatians 2:20—"I am crucified with Christ"—and most directly in 2 Corinthians 5:14—"We thus judge, that if one died for all, then were all dead." This explains why Christ is called "the last Adam." The sinful Adamic race ended when He died (1 Corinthians 15:45). That is why the crucifixion is the solution to sin.

NIGHT

Isaac Watts (1674–1748), the great English hymn writer, composed these words:

> Not all the blood of beasts
> On Jewish altars slain
> Could give the guilty conscience peace
> Or wash away the stain.

> But Christ, the heav'nly Lamb,
> Takes all our sins away;
> A sacrifice of nobler name
> And richer blood than they.

What makes Christ's blood nobler and richer than the sacrifices that God ordained in the Law? Let's view the cross of Christ in the same way as Isaac Watts. He understood that, of all who have ever been born, only Jesus Christ fully pleased God (Romans 8:3–4). Plus, Jesus believed in the goodness of His Father even when it pleased God to make His soul an offering for our sins (Isaiah 53:7–10). The words of Isaac Watts's hymn have a place in the heart of everyone who is justified through the deliverance in Christ (Romans 3:24). That deliverance, which takes place only on the ground of grace, silences all boasting except for our boast in Christ and in God our justifier (Romans 3:26–27).

A person who is justified before God is legally not guilty of sin. This is not the same as forgiveness, which is based on a person's repentance (Acts 2:38). A convicted yet reformed criminal who is forgiven, or pardoned, by a governor is still guilty of his crime though he is freed from its consequences. Moreover, the pardon is only applicable to the one offense. When a believer who is taught that he is forgiven is asked, "Do you sin?" he will say, "Yes, but when I repent, I'm forgiven." But, this does not resolve the problem of his sin. He must maintain good behavior or repent again for his failure. In contrast, justification is based not upon man's repentance but upon God's voluntary favor, because no one deserves it (Romans 3:23–24). Christ Jesus has brought about a deliverance from judgment that is free to all who believe, and that belief is through the faith of Jesus Christ. All this marvelous truth is condensed into this one sentence: "For by grace are ye saved through faith; and that not of yourselves: it is the gift of God" (Ephesians 2:8).

Why all this talk about blood and sin at Christmastime? It can't be avoided. The Son Himself said, "A body you prepared for me"

(Hebrews 10:5 NIV). That is the body of the baby in the manger that grew to be the body of the man on the cross. And that man said, "I have come to do your will, my God" (Hebrews 10:7 NIV). He was perfectly suited to satisfy divine justice.

In the ancient days, the one bringing the sin offering would lay his hand on the head of the sacrifice as it was slain (Leviticus 4:4). Today, what the blood of that creature could not do, the blood of Christ has done and still does. It solves the problem of sin for man and for God. This is why we sing with Isaac Watts,

> My faith would lay her hand
> On that dear head of Thine,
> While, like a penitent, I stand,
> And there confess my sin.

Believing, I rejoice
To see the curse remove;
I bless the Lamb with cheerful voice,
And sing His bleeding love. ❄

December 20

That which was from the beginning,
which we have heard, which we have
seen with our eyes, which we have looked
at and our hands have touched—this we
proclaim concerning the Word of life.
The life appeared; we have seen it and
testify to it, and we proclaim to you the
eternal life, which was with the Father
and has appeared to us. We proclaim to
you what we have seen and heard, so that
you also may have fellowship with us.
And our fellowship is with the Father
and with his Son, Jesus Christ.

1 JOHN 1:1–3 NIV

MORNING

At Christmas we celebrate the beginning of the gospel when the Word became flesh (John 1:1), when "that holy thing" was begotten in Mary (Luke 1:35), and the Savior was born in the city of David (Luke 2:11). This is the moment when the Word of life appeared. Yet this beginning draws us to contemplate another beginning, which is before all beginnings, when the Son was with the Father before the world was (John 17:5).

In that beginning, long before John and the apostles, before the prophets, before Adam and Abraham, and before all creatures, there was someone. Someone existed before the creation of the world. In Him all things were created (Colossians 1:16), and He is from everlasting (Micah 5:2). This is the one whom the Father loved before the foundation of the world (John 17:24) when we were chosen in Him (Ephesians 1:5). He is the perfect Lamb who was known before the foundation of the world and revealed for our sake (1 Peter 1:20). This is the man seen and heard and proclaimed by John, this Word of life, who told him, "Blessed are your eyes because they see, and your ears because they hear. For I tell you, many prophets and righteous people longed to see what you see but did not see it, and to hear what you hear but did not hear it (Matthew 13:16–17 NIV).

Yes, John heard a voice from heaven and saw Christ gloriously transfigured (Matthew 17:2, 5). But even better, he heard Christ's voice in private conversation and in public discourse. He saw His common actions like eating, drinking, walking, and sleeping. He also was there to see Him raise the dead, cleanse the lepers, restore sight to the blind, cause the lame to walk, the dumb to speak, and the deaf to hear. And John saw Jesus hanged upon the cross. He saw the One who is from everlasting bleeding and dying. He heard Him sigh, "It is finished" (John 19:30). John entered the empty tomb after Christ's resurrection from the dead and was with Him for forty days afterward. John was among those who stood and gazed as Jesus Christ, who is from the beginning, was taken up and returned to the Father (Acts 1:9).

NIGHT

The apostles knew the One who was from the beginning. They knew Him very well and were able to describe His stature, features, and the lineaments of His body. Their hands had touched this Word of life.

Peter grasped Christ's hand when he lost faith while walking on water (Matthew 14:29–31). John leaned his head on Jesus' bosom (John 13:23). Thomas, after the resurrection, put his fingers into the Lord's wounds (John 20:27). Similarly, Jesus invited all the apostles to touch him when He appeared to them after His resurrection (Luke 24:39), proving that it was He and not a phantom without flesh and bones.

This Word of life was manifest in the flesh, born in Bethlehem as the Savior, Christ the Lord. We celebrate His birth knowing it was the birth of the author of life (Acts 3:15). But we also celebrate because Jesus does not just belong to those who knew Him during his life on this earth. John proclaimed what he had seen and heard so that we can have fellowship with Him. Thus, He invites us into fellowship with the Father and with His Son, Jesus Christ (1 John 1:3).

The gospel of Jesus Christ is shown during the Christmas season in His marvelous birth. Those who have received the gospel message have been called by God into fellowship with His Son (1 Corinthians 1:9). Fellowship is like a river in which we enjoy the refreshing love of God, the grace of Christ, and the fellowship of the Holy Spirit (2 Corinthians 13:14).

Jesus promised to us the water that takes away thirst altogether and becomes a perpetual spring within us, giving eternal life (John 4:14). One day He even stood up in the Temple and shouted about it: "If anyone thirsts, let him come to Me and drink. He who believes in Me, as the Scripture has said, out of his heart will flow rivers of living water" (John 7:37–38 NKJV). This invitation into the river of God's fellowship continues in the final age when "the Spirit and the bride say, 'Come!'. . . . Whoever desires, let him take the water of life freely" (Revelation 22:17). ❋

December 21

The first man is of the earth, earthy;
the second man is the Lord from heaven.
As is the earthy, such are they also that
are earthy: and as is the heavenly, such
are they also that are heavenly. And as we
have borne the image of the earthy, we
shall also bear the image of the heavenly.

1 Corinthians 15:47–49

MORNING

Think of the biblical images that appear most in popular culture. There are four by my count: Adam and Eve, Noah and the ark, the birth of Jesus, and His death. Adam was the beginning and Noah passed through the judgment of the flood. The birth of Jesus was a new beginning, and in His death He passed through the judgment of the cross. These beginnings cannot be separated from their ends. Likewise, we who know Christ in His birth must know Him in His death.

Scripture also makes an unbreakable link between the two beginnings—that of Adam and that of Christ. Since this is the season to remember the birth of Christ, let's look at the first beginning.

The first man was formed of *dust*, which in

Hebrew signifies *red earth* (Genesis 2:7). Named Adam, meaning *red*, he cared for the Garden and was given dominion over the earth and sea (Genesis 1:26). Then sin entered and Adam was thrust from the Garden to toil in the same earth from which he was taken and for which he was named. "By the sweat of your brow you will eat your food until you return to the ground," said his Creator, "for dust you are and to dust you will return" (Genesis 3:19 NIV).

Everyone born since then must die and return to dust. Adam's sin has pervaded the bodies and souls of all his descendants, making us sensual and earthy—that is, we naturally mind and cleave to earthly things. This explains the popularity of the Christmas season among those who don't believe in Christ. With its parties, gifts, and good food, it is the best time to be like the first man—"of the earth, earthy" (1 Corinthians 15:47).

But the second man is the Lord from heaven. Adam was the first man; Christ is the second. Today's reading from 1 Corinthians speaks of them as if they were the only two men in the world. The first was the head and representative of all his natural offspring. Likewise, the second is the head and representative of all His spiritual offspring.

Formed under the overshadowing of the Holy Spirit out of the substance of Mary, Jesus' body was indeed earthy. It was supported by earthly means, and at its end was interred in the earth. This describes the believer's reason for celebrating Christmas: Christ, the Son of God, was found in fashion as a man (Philippians 2:8).

NIGHT

We observe Christmas because the church has marked this as the time when the second man, the Son of God, "took upon him the form of a servant, and was made in the likeness of men" (Philippians 2:7). Yet there are still two men in this world, one of the earth and the other of heaven—Adam and Christ. Every man and woman is included in one or the other.

Everyone has an earthy body. Just like Adam's, your body is a house of clay. The apostle Paul called his the "earthly house of this tabernacle" (2 Corinthians 5:1). Since its source is Adam, it is formed of the earth, is maintained by the things of the earth, and returns to the earth in death. In other words, "As is the earthy, such are they also that are earthy" (1 Corinthians 15:48), but that's not all, and this is the wonder of

Christmas: "As is the heavenly, such are they also that are heavenly" (1 Corinthians 15:48). Just as you are now physically like Adam, the man of the earth, so you will someday be like Christ, the man from heaven. So, speaking to believers in Christ, scripture says, "Set your minds on things above, not on earthly things. For you died, and your life is now hidden with Christ in God. When Christ, who is your life, appears, then you also will appear with him in glory" (Colossians 3:2–4 NIV).

Christ, the second man, now has a glorious and spiritual body. As certainly as He was born of Mary, He will descend from heaven in His second coming. Your faith in the Lord from heaven makes you a partaker of the heavenly calling (Hebrews 3:1). You are a citizen of heaven (Philippians 3:20 NIV). This means that on that resurrection morning, you will have a heavenly, spiritual, and glorious body like

Christ's (Philippians 3:21).

The following is God's promise given in the birth of Jesus Christ, the second man, the Lord from heaven: "As we have borne the image of the earthy, we shall also bear the image of the heavenly (1 Corinthians 15:49).

For now, we must live in the image of the earthy. But this does not prevent our being rooted and established in love as, through the scriptures, we grasp the width and length and height and depth of Christ. We only bear the image of the first man until we fully know the love that surpasses knowledge and are utterly filled with God (Ephesians 3:17–19). Then we will enjoy deathlessness in a body so changed and glorified that it is compared to the one that is suitable for the head of the universe (Philippians 3:21). ❄

December 22

The book of the generation of Jesus Christ,
the son of David, the son of Abraham.

MATTHEW 1:1

I Jesus have sent mine angel to testify unto
you these things in the churches. I am the
root and the offspring of David, and the
bright and morning star.

REVELATION 22:16

Now to Abraham and his seed were the
promises made. He saith not, And to
seeds, as of many; but as of one, And to
thy seed, which is Christ.

GALATIANS 3:16

Morning

Genesis begins with four chapters that comprise the book of the generation of the world—creation and the birth of human culture. Chapter five of Genesis is called "the book of the generations of Adam" (v. 1). The Gospel of Matthew begins another book that tells of the last Adam (1 Corinthians 15:45). It is titled "the book of the generation of Jesus Christ" (Matthew 1:1). It is the story of the One through whom all things were created, who breathed the breath of life into Adam, was born into the creation, and reconciled all to God.

The story begins with a familiar name—the son of David (Matthew 1:1). Well-educated scribes and Pharisees of that day knew the Messiah by this name, as did the common people (Matthew 12:23; 22:42). But the house of David was buried in obscurity by the time Jesus was born. They could not imagine that the Messiah could actually come out of David's family. Yet their scripture told them, "The LORD hath sworn in truth unto David; he will not turn from it; Of the fruit of thy body will I set upon thy throne. . . . For the Lord hath chosen Zion; he hath desired it for his habitation" (Psalm 132:11, 13). By the time Jesus was born, David had been dead for half a millennium, so the Messiah truly came "as a root out of a dry ground" (Isaiah 53:2).

God said, "I have sworn unto David my servant, Thy seed will I establish for ever, and build up thy throne to all generations" (Psalm 89:3–4). This is a big promise that goes far beyond the little nation of Israel. It concerns the child who would be born and the Son given—the One we adore in the Christmas season. The government of David would rest upon His shoulders (Isaiah 9:6) and His throne is for *all* generations.

NIGHT

Jesus Christ is not only the son of David, but also the son of Abraham (Genesis 17:5). This shows that God is faithful to His promise. So we who read the first sentence of the New Testament can be assured of its fulfillment to the end.

God promised Abraham a son who would be the blessing of the world (Genesis 23:17) The patriarch might have expected this would be his immediate son. But it proved to be the child we revere at Christmastime—born forty-two generations after the promise was given. God fulfilled what was promised long after it was foretold. This excruciating delay in accomplishment of the divine plan exhausted human patience but did not weaken God's promise.

The first few words of the New Testament describe the meaning of all history. They reiterate God's pledge to David of an everlasting kingdom and the guarantee to Abraham of a universal family. We probably won't hear these things mentioned in any Christmas service even though they are the reason the angels could not be restrained on the day of Christ's birth, "saying, Glory to God in the highest, and on earth peace, good will toward men" (Luke 2:13–14).

God's time for the carrying out of His promises came when it was most improbable. The glory of David's kingdom was dull as dust, and Abraham's expectation of a blessed son was two thousand years old. Today we are as distant from the days of Christ as were first-century Jews from the days of Abraham. Scripture foresaw this. Here is the advice it gives:

In the last days scoffers will come, mocking the truth and following their own desires. They will say, "What happened to the promise that Jesus is coming again? From before the times of our ancestors, everything has remained the same since the world was first created". . . . But you must not forget this one thing, dear friends: A day is like a thousand years to the Lord, and a thousand years is like a day. The Lord isn't really being slow about his promise, as some people think. No, he is being patient for your sake. He does not want anyone to be destroyed, but wants everyone to repent.

2 Peter 3:3–4, 8–9 NLT ❋

December 23

And it came to pass in those days, that there went
out a decree from Caesar Augustus that all the world
should be taxed. (And this taxing was first made when
Cyrenius was governor of Syria.) And all went to be
taxed, every one into his own city. And Joseph also
went up from Galilee, out of the city of Nazareth,
into Judaea, unto the city of David, which is called
Bethlehem; (because he was of the house and lineage
of David:) To be taxed with Mary his espoused wife,
being great with child. And so it was, that, while they
were there, the days were accomplished
that she should be delivered.

LUKE 2:1–6

MORNING

Scripture often mentions that God preset a time for Christ to live among us. There was a time for His birth: "When the fulness of the time was come, God sent forth his Son, made of a woman" (Galatians 4:4); a time for Him to preach: Jesus said, "The time is fulfilled, and the kingdom of God is at hand, repent ye, and believe the gospel" (Mark 1:15); a time for His death: "Who gave himself a ransom for all, to be testified in due time" (1 Timothy 2:6); and the right time for the spreading of the gospel: "But hath in due times manifested his word through preaching" (Titus 1:3).

King David prophesied of this, saying, "You will arise and have compassion on Zion, for it is time to show favor to her; the appointed time has come" (Psalm 102:13 NIV). The apostle

Paul called this period "the dispensation of the fulness of times" (Ephesians 1:10). As we observe Christmas, we actually celebrate the coming of the fullness of times.

What if Christ had come immediately after Adam's fall? The enormity of the separation from God would not have been fully realized. We would not have altogether tasted the fruit of sin, experienced our inability to please God, or felt in desperation our need for a Savior. In the fullness of times, sin, death, and impotence were fully developed.

Man's inability to find salvation by obedience to the Law was also manifested. Whether the Law of God or the rule of conscience, it didn't matter—we'd failed. So the moral world was prepared. Plus, the prophecies of various ages centered on this particular time.

Finally, Luke tells that the social and political stage was set for the entrance of the Christ.

Caesar Augustus (63 BC–AD 14) was the second emperor of Rome, inheriting the position in 27 BC from his uncle, Julius Caesar (100–44 BC). His original name, Thurinus, was changed to Augustus, meaning "exalted," after he became Caesar.

Augustus presided over a remarkable twenty years of peace within the empire. This came after an era of vicious civil wars, and so the grateful Romans awarded him the title *Pater Patriae*, "father of his country," in 2 BC. The peace allowed Augustus to decree a census of the empire in order to secure his ability to impose taxes. By the providence of God, a man from Nazareth named Joseph, and his pregnant wife, made their way to Bethlehem in obedience to the decree. There the true Exalted One was born.

NIGHT

About 30 BC, when Caesar Augustus was living in Spain, he intended to take a count of the inhabitants of the empire. But he was distracted from this by disturbances in the realm and his competition with the Roman senate for power. Also, unbeknownst to anyone, this was not the fullness of time. Had the census been taken then, it probably would not have been done later, and the inn at Bethlehem would not have been visited by the couple from Nazareth. But things were ordered by an all-wise providence, "And Joseph also went up from Galilee. . .unto the city of David, which is called Bethlehem. . .to be taxed with Mary his espoused wife" (Luke 2:4–5).

The decree was for the entire world to be taxed. A lot of trouble was taken to accomplish this, though not for the purpose of an earthly kingdom. It was all done to bring a pregnant young woman to the right place at the right time.

Early Christians did not record the date of Christ's birth. The earliest mention of December 25 came in the fourth century. The Eastern Church, centered in Constantinople (now Istanbul, Turkey) at first celebrated Christ's birth in a feast called Epiphany, which means *manifestation*. They chose January 6 as the date for this feast, reasoning that since the first Adam was born on the sixth day of creation, the birth of the last Adam (1 Corinthians 15:45) should be celebrated on the sixth day of the year. The Western Church was centered in Rome. It celebrated Christ's birth on the twenty-fifth of December. The Christian origins of this feast, called *Natalis*, meaning "nativity," are lost to history. Eventually Pope Julius I (337–352) designated December 25

as the proper day. With the coming of the
Reformation, Protestant churches continued
the tradition.

Some Christians complain about the impure
origin of the Christmas celebration. A Pope
chose its date; its decorated trees and wreaths
and a supernatural character named Santa Claus
all have pagan beginnings. But none of this
matters—our faith is what matters. It makes us
sure of what we hope for and certain of what
we do not see (Hebrews 11:1). So, by faith let's
sanctify our hearts with this truth: "When the
fulness of the time was come, God sent forth
his Son, made of a woman" (Galatians 4:4). ❄

December 24

But when Herod was dead, behold, an angel of the Lord appeareth in a dream to Joseph in Egypt, Saying, Arise, and take the young child and his mother, and go into the land of Israel: for they are dead which sought the young child's life. And he arose, and took the young child and his mother, and came into the land of Israel. But when he heard that Archelaus did reign in Judaea in the room of his father Herod, he was afraid to go thither: notwithstanding, being warned of God in a dream, he turned aside into the parts of Galilee: And he came and dwelt in a city called Nazareth: that it might be fulfilled which was spoken by the prophets He shall be called a Nazarene.

MATTHEW 2:19–23

Morning

The Son of God humbled Himself and came to live in the human world. Immediately upon His birth, confusion whirled around Him. Joseph was a good man but could not understand what was happening, so God instructed him through dreams. When danger in Bethlehem threatened the baby Jesus, Joseph took Him to live in Egypt. Acting on another dream, the family returned to Judea. Then, a third dream diverted them to Nazareth. Prophecy said that the Messiah would be born in Bethlehem (Micah 5:2), but everyone knew Him as a Nazarene (Matthew 2:23). How puzzling.

No wonder the disciples gave the wrong answer when Jesus asked, "Who do people say that I am?"

"Some say John the Baptist," they replied,

"some say Elijah, and others say Jeremiah or one of the other prophets" (see Matthew 16:13–14).

People also insultingly called Jesus a drunkard, a friend of sinners, and a criminal. They obviously didn't know who He was. Even the citizens of Jesus' hometown said, "He's just a carpenter's son, and we know Mary, his mother, and his brothers—James, Joseph, Simon, and Judas. All his sisters live right here among us. Where did he learn all these things?" (Matthew 13:55–56 NLT).

The same is true to this day. People simply don't know who Jesus is. What is the remedy for this? When Jesus asked the disciples, "'Who do you say I am?' Simon Peter answered, 'You are the Messiah, the Son of the living God.' Jesus replied, 'You are blessed. . .because my Father in heaven has revealed this to you. You did not learn this from any human being'" (Matthew 16:15–17 NLT).

The story of the baby in the manger did not spring from the human imagination. This event is beyond the grasp of the most refined reasoning. It is something that eye has not seen, nor ear heard, nor has it entered into the mind of man to conceive (1 Corinthians 2:9). The light of nature and force of reason are helpless to understand it.

The gospel is a revelation. Yes, one can understand by the testimony of creation that there is a God—there a seeker can see the living God who gives life and breath and all things to His creatures. But to see that the Son has been given, who was with the Father before the world was, who is the Messiah of Israel and the Savior of the world, is impossible unless the Father reveals it.

NIGHT

I was raised in a family that always went to church. I attended Sunday school and later was active in the youth group, but in all that time, I never saw the true identity of the baby in that manger. One night, when I was twenty-four years old, "It pleased God, who separated me from my mother's womb, and called me by his grace, to reveal his Son in me" (Galatians 1:15–16). Christmas has never been the same for me since then.

The revelation of Christ is the heart of scripture. The Bible says this is "the mystery which hath been hid from ages and from generations, but now is made manifest to his saints. . .which is Christ in you, the hope of glory" (Colossians 1:26–27). This revelation of Christ decodes the Bible. It all makes sense when you see Christ. Even the apostle Paul had to admit, "Though we have known Christ after the flesh, yet now henceforth know we him no more" (2 Corinthians 5:16).

But this is not a one-time event, this revelation of Jesus Christ. As one continues to read and pray in the scriptures, the vision in spirit becomes clearer. Even the apostle John, who saw Christ's life unfold from beginning to end, had not seen it all. When he was an old man he testified, "I was in the Spirit on the Lord's day, and heard behind me a great voice, as of a trumpet, Saying, I am Alpha and Omega, the first and the last: and, What thou seest, write in a book" (Revelation 1:10–11). The book he wrote is the final one in the Bible. It is called The Revelation of Jesus Christ.

Paul prayed for you to have this revelation: "[I] Cease not to give thanks for you, making mention of you in my prayers; That the God of our Lord Jesus Christ, the Father of glory, may give unto you the spirit of wisdom and revelation in the knowledge of him" (Ephesians 1:16–17). If you wish, you can continue Paul's prayer so that Christ will be revealed to yourself and to others:

"Oh, God of my Lord Jesus Christ, Father of glory, give me a spirit of wisdom and revelation in the full knowledge of Your Son. Enlighten the eyes of my understanding so that I can know what is the hope of His calling and what are the riches of the glory of His inheritance in the saints" (see Ephesians 1:18–19). ❉

December 25

Hast thou eaten of the tree, whereof I commanded thee that thou shouldest not eat? And the man said, The woman whom thou gavest to be with me, she gave me of the tree, and I did eat. And the LORD God said unto the woman, What is this that thou hast done? And the woman said, The serpent beguiled me, and I did eat. And the LORD God said unto the serpent, Because thou hast done this, thou art cursed above all cattle, and above every beast of the field; upon thy belly shalt thou go, and dust shalt thou eat all the days of thy life: And I will put enmity between thee and the woman, and between thy seed and her seed; it shall bruise thy head, and thou shalt bruise his heel.

GENESIS 3:11–15

MORNING

Every family has its stories. My aunt recently told my daughter about the tornado in Washington, Kansas. It came through the center of town during a celebration on July 4, 1932, destroying the county courthouse. My aunt took refuge in the fruit cellar of her grandmother's house. When she emerged, the house no longer had a roof and the winds had dropped the water tank from the railroad yard on my great-grandfather's barn.

I treasure my family's stories, though they may have little meaning to anyone else; like the one about my father's dog, Shy Violet, who protected him from rattlesnakes when he was a boy in Oklahoma. The dog was bitten so often that it was immune to the snakes' venom.

The family of man shares many stories. One

tells of Adam's disobedience and the entrance of sin. It resonates with meaning for all humanity, and this meaning is expressed in the Christmas story.

As I reread the account of Genesis 3, it is fresh to me. Like most people, I know that judgment came upon the man and woman after they succumbed to the serpent's temptation. But that's not the first thing that happened— God first promised that the Savior would come, proving for all time that "mercy triumphs over judgment" (James 2:13 NIV). This promise came as God condemned the serpent, saying, "I will put enmity between thee and the woman, and between thy seed and her seed; it shall bruise thy head, and thou shalt bruise his heel" (Genesis 3:15).

Within these words are found all the truths that make up the gospel of Christ. At first glance this is hard to see. But, just as oak tree lies within an acorn, likewise, the mystery of Christ is revealed here—He is the seed of the woman. This promised seed was all that Adam had by way of revelation of God's purpose. Surely he passed this hope on to his sons, and Abel believed. By this light, Abel brought the firstborn of his flock and laid them on an altar, and his murder proved that the seed of the serpent hated the seed of the woman.

Thereafter every generation of believers died without receiving the promised salvation, though by faith they saw it from a distance. Is it too much to expect that our generation would thank God every day that *unto us* was born the Savior who is Christ the Lord?

Night

I will put enmity between thee and the woman, and between thy seed and her seed; it shall bruise thy head, and thou shalt bruise his heel" (Genesis 3:15). At first glance this text looks hard. And it is hard, like a seed out of which grows grace and truth: "A virgin shall conceive, and bear a son, and shall call his name Immanuel" (Isaiah 7:14).

The two seeds of Genesis 3:15 are seen in Cain and Abel, Isaac and Ishmael, Jacob and Esau, even David and Goliath. So we are informed, "But as then he that was born after the flesh persecuted him that was born after the Spirit, even so it is now" (Galatians 4:29). The enmity or hostility between these two seeds has found its way into your own heart where "the flesh lusteth against the Spirit, and the Spirit against the flesh: and these are contrary the one to the other" (Galatians 5:17).

In the garden, God told the serpent of the coming seed of the woman: "It shall bruise thy head" (Genesis 3:15). This foretells the accomplishment of all things—the breaking of Satan's power and the destruction of sin in Christ's death, the abolishment of death by resurrection, the liberation of captivity in the ascension, and the victory of truth through the coming of the Spirit. It gives hope for the day in which Satan will be bound and when the evil one is cast into the lake of fire. These few words, "It shall bruise thy head," tell not only of the conflict but also of the conquest. They may not have been fully understood by those who first heard them, but to us, for whom the mystery is revealed, they are full of light.

Adam gave names to all the animals, but when God presented the woman, she was not given a name. Soon the couple failed, but only then heard the good news: They would not immediately die, as they supposed (Genesis 2:17). There would be a seed of the woman! Though he was cursed, Adam immediately turned to the woman and called her Eve, "Because she was the mother of all living" (Genesis 3:20).

Our revelation of Christ as compared to that of Adam is like the brightness of the sun to a distant star, and it is the wonder of Christmas. We see that the baby in the manger grew up to be our Redeemer—the seed of the woman came! "O the depth of the riches both of the wisdom and knowledge of God! how unsearchable are his judgments, and his ways past finding out!" (Romans 11:33). ❄

Scripture Index

About the Author

Daniel Partner, a veteran Christian author and editor, lives in Coos Bay, Oregon. His books include *I Give Myself to Prayer*, *All Things Are Possible*, *Peace Like a River*, *Women of Sacred Song* (written with his wife Margaret), and most recently, *365 Daily Devotions from Favorite Hymns*. Contact him by e-mail at author@danpartner.com.